AGRICULTURAL AND URBAN AREAS

Peter D. Moore

Illustrations by
Richard Garratt

CHELSEA HOUSE
PUBLISHERS
An imprint of Infobase Publishing

From Peter D. Moore:
To Eunice, Helen, and Caroline

From Richard Garratt: To Chantal,
who has lightened my darkness

Agricultural and Urban Areas

Chelsea House
An imprint of Infobase Publishing
132 West 31st Street
New York NY 10001

Library of Congress Cataloging-in-Publication Data
Moore, Peter D.
    Agricultural and urban areas / Peter D. Moore; illus. by Richard Garratt.
        p. cm.—(Biomes of the Earth)
    Includes bibliographical references and index.
    ISBN 0-8160-5326-X
    1. Agriculture—Environmental aspects. 2. Urban ecology. I. Title. II. Series.
    S589.75.M66 2006
    333.7—dc22   2005007912

Chelsea House books are available at special discounts when purchased in bulk quantities for businesses, associations, institutions, or sales promotions. Please call our Special Sales Department in New York at (212) 967-8800 or (800) 322-8755.

You can find Chelsea House on the World Wide Web at http://www.chelseahouse.com

Text design by David Strelecky
Cover design by Cathy Rincon
Illustrations by Richard Garratt
Photo research by Elizabeth H. Oakes

Printed in China

CP FOF 10 9 8 7 6 5 4 3 2 1

This book is printed on acid-free paper.

CONTENTS

CHAPTER 4
BIODIVERSITY IN FARMS AND CITIES

CHAPTER 5
THE HISTORY AND PREHISTORY OF FARMS AND CITIES

CHAPTER 6
AGRICULTURAL AND URBAN CONSERVATION

176

PREFACE

Earth is a remarkable planet. There is nowhere else in our solar system where life can survive in such a great diversity of forms. As far as we can currently tell, our planet is unique. Isolated in the barren emptiness of space, here on Earth we are surrounded by a remarkable range of living things, from the bacteria that inhabit the soil to the great whales that migrate through the oceans, from the giant redwood trees of the Pacific forests to the mosses that grow on urban sidewalks. In a desolate universe, Earth teems with life in a bewildering variety of forms.

One of the most exciting things about the Earth is the rich pattern of plant and animal communities that exists over its surface. The hot, wet conditions of the equatorial regions support dense rain forests with tall canopies occupied by a wealth of animals, some of which may never touch the ground. The cold, bleak conditions of the polar regions, on the other hand, sustain a much lower variety of species of plants and animals, but those that do survive under such harsh conditions have remarkable adaptations to their testing environment. Between these two extremes lie many other types of complex communities, each well suited to the particular conditions of climate prevailing in its region. Scientists call these communities *biomes*.

The different biomes of the world have much in common with one another. Each has a plant component, which is responsible for trapping the energy of the Sun and making it available to the other members of the community. Each has grazing animals, both large and small, that take advantage of the store of energy found within the bodies of plants. Then come the predators, ranging from tiny spiders that feed upon even smaller insects to tigers, eagles, and polar bears that survive by preying upon large animals. All of these living things form a complicated network of feeding interactions, and, at the base of the system, microbes in the soil are ready to consume the energy-rich plant litter or dead animal flesh that remains. The biome, then, is an integrated unit within which each species plays its particular role.

This set of books aims to outline the main features of each of the Earth's major biomes. The biomes covered include the tundra habitats of polar regions and high mountains, the taiga (boreal forest) and temperate forests of somewhat warmer lands, the grasslands of the prairies and the tropical savanna, the deserts of the world's most arid locations, and the tropical forests of the equatorial regions. The wetlands of the world, together with river and lake habitats, do not lie neatly in climatic zones over the surface of the Earth but are scattered over the land. And the oceans are an exception to every rule. Massive in their extent, they form an interconnecting body of water extending down into unexplored depths, gently moved by global currents.

Humans have had an immense impact on the environment of the Earth over the past 10,000 years since the last Ice Age. There is no biome that remains unaffected by the presence of the human species. Indeed, we have created our own biome in the form of agricultural and urban lands, where people dwell in greatest densities. The farms and cities of the Earth have their own distinctive climates and natural history, so they can be regarded as a kind of artificial biome that people have created, and they are considered as a separate biome in this set.

Each biome is the subject of a separate volume. Each richly illustrated book describes the global distribution, the climate, the rocks and soils, the plants and animals, the history, and the environmental problems found within each biome. Together, the set provides students with a sound basis for understanding the wealth of the Earth's biodiversity, the factors that influence it, and the future dangers that face the planet and our species.

Is there any practical value in studying the biomes of the Earth? Perhaps the most compelling reason to understand the way in which biomes function is to enable us to conserve their rich biological resources. The world's productivity is the basis of the human food supply. The world's biodiversity holds a wealth of unknown treasures, sources of drugs and medicines that will help to improve the quality of life. Above all, the world's biomes are a constant source of wonder, excitement, recreation, and inspiration that feed not only our bodies but also our minds and spirits. These books aim to provide the information about biomes that readers need in order to understand their function, draw upon their resources, and, most of all, enjoy their diversity.

ACKNOWLEDGMENTS

I should like to record my gratitude to the editorial staff at Chelsea House for their untiring support, assistance, and encouragement during the preparation of this book. Frank K. Darmstadt, executive editor, has been a constant source of advice and information, and Dorothy Cummings, project editor, has edited the text with unerring skill and impeccable care. I am grateful to you both. I should also like to thank Richard Garratt for his excellent illustrations and Elizabeth Oakes for her perceptive selection of photographs. I have also greatly appreciated the help and guidance of Mike Allaby, my fellow author at Chelsea House. Thanks to my wife, who has displayed a remarkable degree of patience and support during the writing of this book, together with much needed critical appraisal, and to my daughters, Helen and Caroline, who have supplied ideas and materials that have enriched the text. I must also acknowledge the contribution of many generations of students in the Life Sciences Department of the University of London, King's College, who have been a constant source of stimulation and who will recall (I trust) many of the ideas contained here. Thanks are also due to my colleagues in teaching and research, especially those who have accompanied me on field courses and research visits to many parts of the world. Their work underlies the science presented in this book.

INTRODUCTION

There is not a single part of the land surface of the Earth that is unaffected by human activity. Even the wildest parts of Antarctica and the open deserts of the Sahara have upon them the mark of humankind. There may not be footprints on the ground, but we can leave our imprints in many other ways. People have altered the chemical composition of the atmosphere to such an extent that they have begun to modify the climate of the whole world. Chemical waste products are now so abundant in the environment and destructive pesticides so widely dispersed that even Antarctic penguins carry traces of them in their body fat. The oceans are littered with trash and with oil that has been carelessly spilled. Only the very deepest areas of the ocean bed, where submarine volcanoes belch out their black smoke, can one still find animals that remain blissfully ignorant of and uncontaminated by the human presence on Earth.

The impact of people on most of the world's land surface is only too apparent; we have only to look out of the window of the room where we are currently sitting to observe the extent of human influence. Whether in a city school, or home, or office, the entire surrounding landscape is human constructed. Cliffs of concrete rise out of the ground, the surface of which is covered by reconstituted rocks formed into paving slabs and road surfaces. Perhaps some trees or grass are visible, but the chances are that people have planted them and maintain them according to their own tastes and fancies. It is very likely that the plants seen in gardens and city streets have originated in distant parts of the world and have been brought to town because of their exotic appeal or because these plants are prepared to put up with the drought, the dust, and the pollution of streets and highways. Perhaps a bird flies past the window, a pigeon, a starling, or an English sparrow.

Even these have been imported. The rock doves of Europe were the ancestors of our urban pigeons. They once inhabited the cliffs of western Europe and the Mediterranean but long ago became adapted to the artificial cliffs of ancient cities. They were brought over to North America by the early settlers, perhaps to remind them of home, but also to provide a very handy source of pigeon pie. Similarly, but less tasty, the starling and the English sparrow (really a weaver finch) are also Old World birds introduced by human migrants. Both birds and people spread successfully across the North American continent. So we really have built a world around ourselves in cities and have brought along our own fellow urban creatures to make us feel at home.

The countryside may appear more natural, but appearances can be deceptive. The crops in agricultural fields have almost all been brought from distant locations, such as corn from Mexico and wheat from western Asia, likewise the domestic animals, including cows from Europe and chickens from Southeast Asia. Even the weeds in gardens and arable fields are largely imported. So we have brought together a strange mixture of plants and animals in our cities and farms, some of which are the original inhabitants of the land we have changed, such as the crows, crickets, and raccoons, but many of which we have brought in from far away. The natural vegetation of farmland areas has been altered beyond recognition. Just fragments remain where woodlots or grassland have not been plowed.

People have effectively created completely new ecosystems, indeed a whole new biome that has characteristics quite different from all others. The great cities of the world, among them Tokyo, New York, Delhi, São Paulo, London, Los Angeles, Beijing, and Rome, all have similar problems and have much in common in their wildlife and its adaptations. The farms of the world, whether the banana plantations of Uganda, the rice paddies of Vietnam, or the cornfields of America, are all human-manipulated ecosystems that are gathering the energy of the Sun through the process of plant photosynthesis and converting it into food to supply the populations of cities. So the town and the country have evolved together and are closely linked together in a global web.

In these days of rapid transport and easy communication, this created biome is perhaps the most intact and integrated of them all. It is also the most recently developed of all of the Earth's biomes. The tropical rain forests originated in the deep mists of ancient time, more than 100 million years ago. The tundra biome must have arisen with the raising of the great mountain chains, such as the Alps and the Himalayas, and spread with the cooling of the planet around 50 million years ago. The tropical grasslands, or savannas, extended as the grasses diversified and multiplied around 20 million years ago. But the agricultural and urban landscapes only began their evolution some 10,000 years ago as the human species began to manipulate the environment and to create habitats suitable for its survival and success. Of all other living organisms, only ants, termites, and beetles had struck upon the notion of cultivating other organisms, caring for them, and diverting their produce to the support of society. These tiny creatures have developed systems of cultivating fungi, supplying them with vegetable matter so that the fibrous cellulose can be degraded and converted into digestible sugars for the colony to harvest, or herding aphids (tiny plant-feeding insects) and milking them for their honeydew secretions. Like humans, these insects also live in large gatherings with complex social structures, the cities of the insect world. So we are not the first inhabitants of the Earth to hit upon the idea of farming or city dwelling, for some insects had followed this strategy some 40 to 60 million years ago. But when humans began to develop farms and cities, they changed the entire face of the planet.

Where did it all begin?

The origins of human farming are to be found way back at the end of the last major glacial episode on the face of the Earth, around 10,000 years ago, when the climate became rapidly warmer and our species, *Homo sapiens,* emerged dominant among the hominids. Neanderthal man, a separate species that had accompanied us into the glacial some 50,000 years previously, failed to survive. Intelligence, adaptability, and inventiveness were the most important characteristics of our ancestors, and undoubtedly it was these features that led to the domestication of the wolf for aid in hunting and then the development of the idea of collecting the seeds of wild grasses, sowing them, protecting them, and ultimately breeding crops from them. With this new idea of agriculture came the need to change the environment, because the crop plants would not grow beneath woodland canopies, and our ancestors found plowed soils with added manure ideal for high productivity. So began the long process of humans trying to manage the natural world and bring its great productive forces into the support of our species.

The idea of agriculture did not arise just once in a single area of the world but seems to have been developed independently at many times and in many places. Wheat, barley, flax, plums, and carrots came from Syria and the Middle East; peas, beans, and lentils came from the western Mediterranean; millet, soybeans, spinach, garlic, and almonds came from central and western Asia; rice, sugarcane, cotton, and bananas came from southeast Asia; and from the New World came peppers, corn (maize), squashes, tomatoes, potatoes, tobacco, peanuts, and pineapples. Yet despite this list of cultivated plants brought into the service of humankind throughout the world, just three species account for half of the world's crop production, and 96 percent of production comes from only 15 species of plant. Following the great innovation of plant domestication many thousands of years ago, we seem to have become satisfied and complacent about what has been achieved, and very few other plant or animal species have subsequently been added to our agricultural resources.

With the arrival of agriculture and the relative security of food supply that it offered, the nomadic hunting and gathering style of life was no longer necessary. Families could settle in one place, in small communities, and develop an orderly and organized way of life. Thus began the process that led to the formation of towns and cities, which eventually became almost parasitic on the countryside as they absorbed the nourishment that the farmers produced. As society became more complex and as industrial processes were developed, so the cities became bigger and their inhabitants had less and less contact with the countryside that supported them. Urbanization, the concentration of increasing proportions of the population into the cities, had begun, and it has continued to the present time.

Taking over the world

We shall never know how many people there were in the world when the agricultural revolution began. One thing we can be sure of, however, is that there were far fewer than are found on Earth today. Our early ancestors made a living by gathering the wild produce of the land: seeds and fruits, tubers from the ground. The hunting of game and the gathering of honey, grubs, and birds' eggs would have added to the diet of early human groups, but even in a productive part of the world, such as the tropical rain forest, the numbers of people that could be supported in this way would have been small. There are still some hunter/gatherer communities living in the world, such as the Bushmen of the Kalahari Desert in southern Africa, and it is known that this way of life can support a density of only about one person in 640 acres (260 ha). Compare this with a modern society of farmland and cities, where one person can be supported on less than 2.5

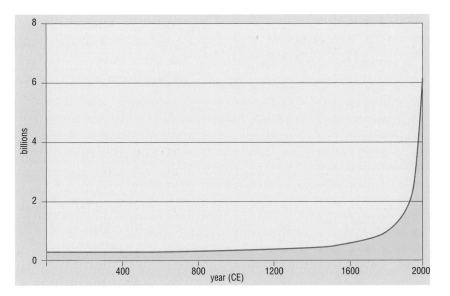

The rising human population of the world over the last 2,000 years

acres (1 ha). This means that the gradual development of agriculture and its associated city dwelling allowed human populations to expand (see the figure on page xix). As they expanded, the impact they made upon the natural environment became stronger and more widespread.

As populations grew, the people dispersed to new regions, taking the idea of agriculture with them. From the Middle East, for example, there was a movement of people into Europe, northern Africa, and Northwest Asia. It took about 5,000 years for the new agricultural technology to reach Britain and Scandinavia. Was this a movement of people, or just the spread of an idea? Archaeologists have long debated this question. Recent evidence from the genetics of modern humans in Europe and the Middle East suggest that it was the people who moved. The agricultural communities contained as many as 70 percent new immigrants from the south.

In North America, hunting peoples had moved from Asia across the land bridge that linked what is now Russia with Alaska across the Bering Sea, and they had spread across the Americas. Quite independently of the developments in Asia and Europe, these people established an agriculture based on native plants, such as corn, beans, squashes, and peppers. The earliest date for this agriculture is again around 10,000 years ago, coinciding with the birth of the agricultural idea in the Middle East. The pattern of agricultural spread is less well marked in North America than in Europe, but it is possible to trace the spread of corn cultivation up the eastern seaboard of the continent from Mexico, and it is likely that population levels expanded as this new way of life became widespread.

Australia has long been occupied by people, but the agricultural revolution did not arrive there until late, with the "discovery" of the region by people of European origin. From around 400 C.E., the islands of the South Pacific were gradually occupied by seafaring populations carrying crop plants and livestock in outrigger canoes. The Maori people reached New Zealand only about 1,000 years ago. By this time, human beings had spread over all parts of the Earth that were capable of supporting them (see the map), and the human species had become by far the most dominant and influential organism on the planet.

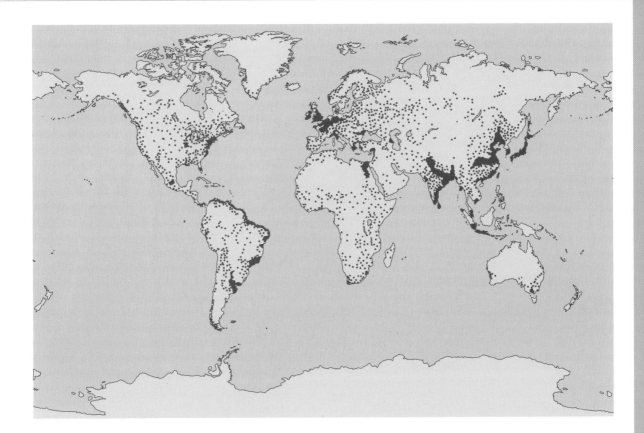

Disease, industrialization, and intensive agriculture

Agriculture allowed human populations to grow, but there were other factors that prevented a population explosion. Warfare was one such factor, but by far the most important control on human population levels was disease. Food supply and disease are closely linked because underfed people are more subject to infection than are the well nourished. When people began to associate together in towns and cities, they added to the risk by assisting in the spread of infectious and contagious diseases, among them smallpox, bubonic plague, and measles.

The movements of armies, sailors, and traders brought new diseases to people unaccustomed to their impact and unprotected by immunity. The Black Death (bubonic plague), which swept through Asia and Europe in the 14th century, has been estimated to have killed 20 percent of the population of Europe, reckoned to be about 100 million people at

The distribution of the world's human population. The density of red stippling on the map indicates the density of settlement.

that time. This disease was spread by the black rat, an animal that was very content to share city life with humans. So the opportunities for population expansion that agriculture brought were soon constrained by the diseases that spread rapidly in the communities of cities.

The development of industry added to the problems of the spread of disease. The high density of dwellings that accompanied industrial expansion, and the poverty and poor diet often associated with the working population, led to the rapid spread of such diseases as cholera and tuberculosis, which continued to ravage societies well into the 20th century. Though it may have helped spread disease, industry also provided a stimulus to population growth. The invention of the internal combustion engine, for example, brought a powerful new tool to the farmer. It is difficult now to envisage farming without tractors and other motorized vehicles, but until very recently the power of the horse and the ox were all that was available to break the sod and turn the soil. Another great leap forward was the development of a technique for "fixing" atmospheric nitrogen, that is, converting this needed element to a form readily taken up by plants. Artificial nitrogen fixation led to a revolution in chemical fertilizers, and around 40 percent of the world's population is currently dependent on this process. Crop and animal breeding techniques have also improved the efficiency of agriculture, and further developments in genetic engineering will accelerate the rate at which new breeds can be developed. All of these processes have also brought environmental problems that need to be solved, but there is no doubt that they have led to increasing human populations, bigger cities, more land brought into agricultural production, and a spread of human influence throughout the globe.

Where will it all end?

The accelerating spread of human domination of the planet, coupled with the accelerating human population growth as disease and food supply problems are solved, must prompt the question where it will lead in the future. In 1950 there were about 2.5 billion people on Earth. By 1970 this had risen to 3.6 billion. The 6 billion mark was passed in the

1990s (see the figure on page xix), and the United Nations projects that the world population will be about 10 billion by 2050 and 11.6 billion in 2150, which is almost a doubling of the current global population. The bulk of the population increase over the next 150 years will be in the developing world.

Is there a limit to how many people the Earth can support? In 1697 Antoni van Leeuwenhoek (1632–1723), the inventor of the microscope, tried to calculate this value, and he came to the conclusion that a maximum of 13.4 billion people could survive on the planet. More recently a number of attempts have been made to estimate possible sustainable human population levels, given the limited resources of the planet. Several factors could limit how many people the Earth can support, such as the amount of food energy that can be produced, the amount of freshwater that will be available, or even the presence of enough mineral elements, such as phosphorus, that will be needed. One calculation indicates that 40 percent of the energy trapped by the photosynthesis of the world's vegetation is already diverted into human sustenance, so even if it were possible to catch most of the rest, the population could do no more than double. The population expert Joel E. Cohen claims that the Earth could sustain 10 billion people, but only if everyone adopted a vegetarian diet and consumed a maximum of 2,500 calories a day per person. This is very unlikely to happen.

The next few decades will put these predictions to the test. Can we stabilize population growth? And can we support the population that has been attained by that stage? Are we approaching the carrying capacity of the Earth for human beings? And if so, what can be done about it? To answer these very important questions, a clear understanding is needed of how the agricultural and urban biome functions.

First, it is necessary to look at global patterns of agriculture and the reasons why these patterns have developed. Then, the distribution of cities around the world must be examined to see why they are located in these positions and how they have grown and evolved their own structure. The rocks that lie beneath farms and cities have influenced farming practice and the structural form of cities. Both farms and cities can be considered ecosystems, and this view proves a valuable way of investigating how they work and how the two ecosystems interact with each other. The plants and animals that share farms and cities with their human inhabitants display some complex adaptations to their adopted environment, and these organisms provide agricultural and urban areas with a distinctive biodiversity. The history and prehistory of farming and city dwelling have much to teach us about how people came to develop the modern way of life. Finally, it is necessary to look at the future of agriculture and the cities. Climate is changing, but so is technology. Both agriculture and the urban way of life will need to alter to cope with a rapidly changing world. That is what this book is all about.

GEOGRAPHY OF FARMS AND CITIES

Farms and cities are habitats made by people and for the use of people. Their geography over the face of the Earth, unlike that of the other great biomes and habitats, is therefore dependent upon human choices. Farms and cities are found only where human beings live and in locations where humans choose to place them. Agricultural lands are further limited in their distribution by the demands of the domesticated plants and animals that accompany us and support our populations by supplying us with food. Although human beings are very adaptable animals, there are still many parts of the world where living is so difficult that it is simply not worth the effort. The frozen regions, including Arctic Canada, Arctic Russia, and Antarctica, and the great deserts of the world have low human population densities because it is so difficult to make a living and to survive comfortably in these regions. Those people who manage to occupy such regions are often involved in hunting and/or gathering of food or are dependent on food supplies coming from elsewhere. Food production using agriculture is even more limited in its geographical extent than the range of humans over the planet; this is because the crop plants and many of the domesticated animals are less adaptable and more sensitive to climate than the human beings they serve. So the distribution of people around the world is strongly influenced by the demands of our domesticated animals and plants.

Where are the farmlands?

Agriculture is possible only where the plants and animals we use can survive and thrive, but the different species we exploit have different requirements. Generally, animals are more adaptable than plants. Moreover, just as we can modify

1

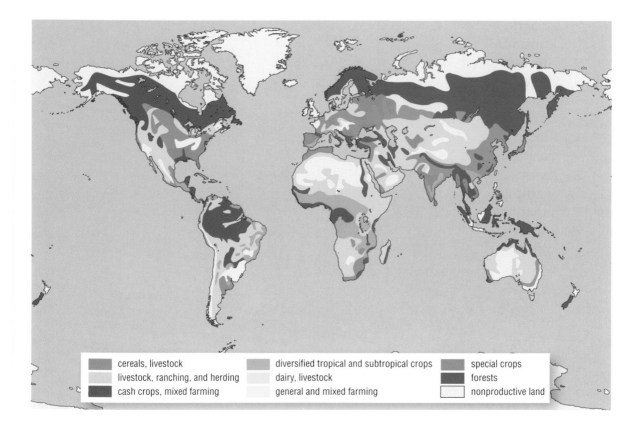

cereals, livestock
livestock, ranching, and herding
cash crops, mixed farming
diversified tropical and subtropical crops
dairy, livestock
general and mixed farming
special crops
forests
nonproductive land

Global distribution of different types of agriculture around the world

our own environment to make it more comfortable by building houses and changing the conditions that immediately surround us, so we can protect animals from adverse climatic conditions. In the harsh winters of high mountain regions, for example, animals can be housed in the winter and provided with stored food so that they do not have to endure the worst of the winter conditions. The same is true to some extent for plants; we can build greenhouses to protect them from the cold, and we can supplement their water supply in dry conditions. But animal husbandry can usually be practiced in more severe climates and under poorer soil conditions than plant cultivation.

Agricultural systems are distributed in a distinctive pattern around the world, as is shown in the map. Apart from the absence of agricultural activity in the nonproductive parts of the world, such as the tundra and desert regions, there are also extensive forests still remaining that have not yet been cleared for agriculture. These are mainly situated in the equatorial regions, where some rain forests still survive intact, and also in the boreal regions just to the south of the Arctic Circle, where coniferous forests are often managed and harvested by humans but have not yet been cleared for arable or pastoral agriculture. Apart from these two areas, as the map shows, human beings have brought a large proportion of the land surface of the Earth into agricultural production. One estimate is that 47 percent of the land surface could be cultivated (meaning that climatic and soil conditions would be appropriate for agriculture), but only 26 percent of that available area actually has been brought into a managed and cultivated state. The map on page 2 does not indicate how intensively agriculture takes place within each of the regions shown. In most areas, agriculture is patchy and there are numerous, sometimes extensive areas of natural or seminatural vegetation surviving. These are areas that have the potential for more productive agriculture, but, on the other hand, such developments would be likely to reduce the conservation value of such regions and this could result in the reduction of biodiversity. We need agriculture to feed the world, but there is a strict limit to how much space is available, and using all of that space for food production would have important implications for the maintenance of the world's resource of wild animals and plants (see "The value of biodiversity," pages 176–179).

What are the underlying causes of the global pattern of farming activity? Why are some regions characterized by livestock farming and others by mixed or plant-based agriculture? The pattern is easier to understand if we examine the map on page 4 devoted to the general distribution of plant production over the land surface of the planet. Plant growth is controlled by a number of different factors. Plants need light to conduct the process of photosynthesis, the biochemical mechanism by which they convert the energy of sunlight into the chemical energy of sugars and storage compounds such as starch. But the actual intensity of light is rarely the limiting factor for photosynthesis. Normal daylight, even at high latitudes, is usually more than sufficient to saturate the biochemical system by which the light is trapped and put to

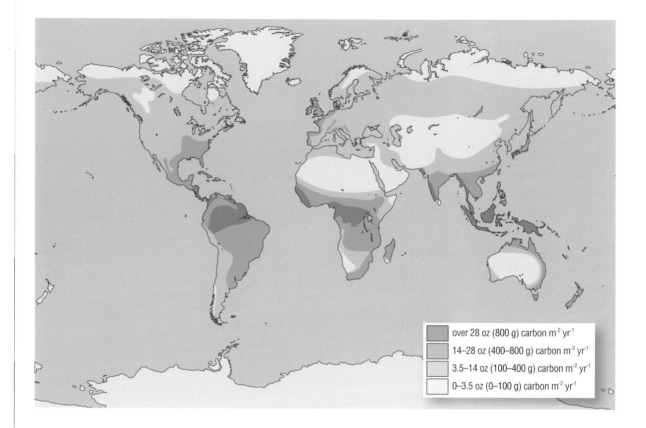

■	over 28 oz (800 g) carbon m^{-2} yr^{-1}
▨	14–28 oz (400–800 g) carbon m^{-2} yr^{-1}
▧	3.5–14 oz (100–400 g) carbon m^{-2} yr^{-1}
□	0–3.5 oz (0–100 g) carbon m^{-2} yr^{-1}

The distribution of plant productivity over the Earth's land surface, measured in annual accumulation of carbon

use. Only beneath the dense shade of other plants or in the entrances to caves is light intensity likely to be limiting on land. The length of day, however, can cause problems, particularly when it becomes extremely short, or even absent, as in a polar winter.

Temperature is important to all chemical reactions, and those taking place within plants are no exception. Low temperatures in winter slow the rate of activity of plants, so plant productivity tends to drop off toward the poles. The low temperature can also make it difficult for the plant to take up water. This means that plants in temperate regions can become drought stressed in winter, which is why many trees lose their leaves in the fall. Water availability is also a problem for plant growth in certain tropical parts of the world. With increasing distance from the equator toward the tropics of Capricorn and Cancer, there is a longer period in the year when water is in short supply. If a plant runs short of water it responds by closing up the pores in its leaves. But these pores are the means by which the gas carbon dioxide is taken up from the atmosphere and converted into more complex molecules, such as sugars, using the energy derived from sunlight. So when a plant becomes short of water and closes its pores, it also cuts down on how much photosynthesis can take place. In other words, it reduces its productivity. As the map shows, productivity in Africa declines progressively between the equator and the northern part of the continent where the Sahara lies, and this is related to the decline in water availability.

There is also the question of how long the growing season lasts. High latitudes (regions closer to the poles) have bigger differences between the seasons. At the equator there is very little change in weather conditions through the year, but at high latitudes there may be wide seasonal alterations in conditions. This may take the form of wet and dry seasons, as in the zones immediately to the north and south of the equator, or it may result in hot and cold seasons, as in the temperate regions, especially in the middle of continental landmasses. When seasonal changes are strong, there may be a distinct growing season, when the domesticated crops are able to be productive, alternating with a season in which growth does not take place. The length of the growing season may determine what crops can be grown. In the case of corn (maize), for example, it is the mature fruit (cob) that is the main crop. This fruit needs lengthy conditions of warm weather to ripen, so there is a limit to how far north it can be grown for the production of cobs. Farther north, the plant produces vegetative growth but the fruit does not mature within the limited season.

There is one further factor that affects global plant productivity, namely the quality of the soil. Plants obtain carbon from the atmosphere, and this is the major element (apart from hydrogen and oxygen) needed for the accumulation of energy-rich materials. But other elements are needed for additional types of biochemical molecules. Proteins contain nitrogen, nucleic acids and cell membranes contain phosphorus, and various cell processes require such elements as potassium and calcium, to name but a few. These have to be acquired from the soil, so if the soil is poor in any of the elements that are needed, plant growth and productivity are held back. Soil poverty, therefore, can be a deterrent to arable agriculture (see "Soil conditions and plant growth," pages 43–51). In practice, the climate (mainly the temperature and the availability of water) imposes certain broad limits on arable agriculture and prevents agricultural development in the polar regions and the deserts, but within the climatic possibilities, it is soil quality that controls whether cultivation can take place. In the tropical regions of South America and Africa, for example, the climatic conditions for arable agriculture are good, but the soils are generally too poor to produce good yields. Of these two areas, only in eastern Africa, where volcanic activity in the past has enriched the soils, is the soil quality good enough for high crop productivity. In India, on the other hand, the soils are good, but the climate is too dry for optimal crop production.

When the conditions are not ideal for arable farming, animal husbandry tends to take over. Livestock production also has its limits, however. Grazing animals still depend on plant

Arable agriculture in a South European village. Vines are grown on the sunny hill slopes, creating a diverse landscape. (Courtesy of Fogstock)

productivity for their livelihood, so when that productivity drops too low, the grazing becomes inefficient and uneconomical. Northern Africa illustrates this limitation. Grazing can be sustained while plant productivity exceeds three ounces of carbon being fixed by photosynthesis in each square yard each year (equivalent to 100 g/m^2), but if the productivity of the vegetation drops below this then grazing becomes increasingly difficult to sustain. There is a similar problem of limitation when the growing season of the plants is limited by cold winters. In the cool temperate zone, for example, grasses may cease growth during the winter because of cold conditions. To continue grazing animals on a field where there is no vegetation growth could result in the destruction of the grass cover, depending on the intensity of the grazing. The alternative is for the farmer to store surplus fodder during the growing season and supplement the feed for the animals during the winter.

It can be seen, therefore, that the patterns of farmlands across the face of the Earth are determined largely by environmental conditions, especially by temperature, rainfall, and soils. In fact, this is precisely the same as can be observed in the natural biomes, such as tropical rain forest, savanna grasslands, boreal forests, temperate grasslands, and so on. In that respect, our agricultural systems are subject to precisely the same biogeographical rules that govern the natural world. Since we are using the domesticated versions of once-wild animals and plants as a basis for our agriculture, this is perhaps not surprising.

Where are the cities?

The rules underlying the distribution of the world's urban settlements are quite different. From the map of the distribution of the largest cities in the world, on page 8, there is no obvious close correlation with plant productivity or climate. Yet it is true that the regions of the world that are least supportive of agriculture (the ice caps, tundra, and deserts) are also virtually devoid of cities. There are exceptions, such as Salt Lake City, Utah, and Las Vegas, Nevada, but these are unusual cities in many respects. Cities, therefore, evidently need certain

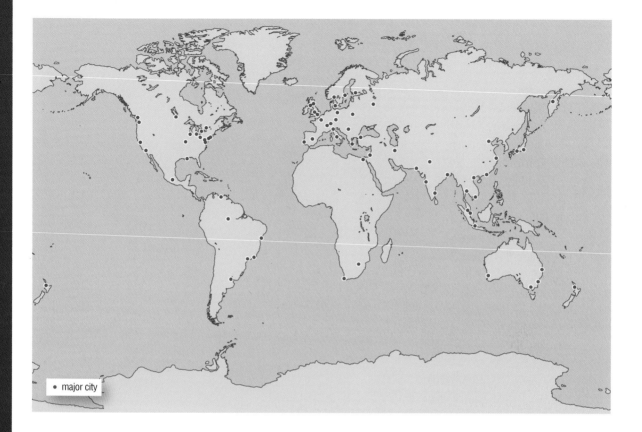

- major city

The locations of the major cities of the world. Note how many are established in coastal regions. Many of the remaining inland cities are found on major rivers.

minimum resources to support them. Food supply is an obvious resource that all cities require, which accounts for the scarcity of cities in regions of very low agricultural productivity. But food supply may not be the determining factor in the location of cities. Other resources may be equally or more important. The city of Johannesburg in South Africa, for example, was established because of the mineral wealth, particularly diamonds, in the surrounding area. The city of Palm Springs, California, has clean desert air as one of its major attractions, and Las Vegas combines this attribute with a history of recreational activities. So, some cities have unexpected resources quite apart from agricultural ones.

Very many of the large cities of the world are coastal or are linked to the coast by rivers. New York, Los Angeles, London, Singapore, Tokyo, Rome, Rio de Janeiro, Sydney, Cape Town, and Buenos Aires are all great coastal cities. There are exceptions, of course, such as Mexico City and Beijing, but most of

Storms and tsunamis

Human settlements along coastal regions are prone to certain risks that are not experienced by settlements inland. Storms, especially when coupled with very high tides, can result in flooding and damage to low-lying coastal areas. In the temperate regions, deep depressions are accompanied by strong winds that circulate around a center of low pressure, spinning clockwise in the Northern Hemisphere and counterclockwise in the Southern Hemisphere. These winds create strong wave action, especially when they cross extensive areas of ocean before striking the shore. The east coast of the United States is especially prone to such storms, as is the west of Europe. In the North Sea region, its funnel shape exacerbates the problem, southward-moving waters being forced into the constricted sea between Denmark, Germany, and the Netherlands in the east, and the British Isles in the west. When storms accompany high tides in this region they frequently flood the low-lying coasts, including villages and towns. Even large cities such as Amsterdam and London are under constant threat of flooding.

Tropical storms, or typhoons, are even more ferocious, generating higher wind speeds. Regions such as the Caribbean and the Gulf of Mexico, or the Bay of Bengal in the north of the Indian Ocean are particularly prone to such storms and the flooding of coastal settlements.

Tidal waves, or tsunamis, are even more devastating. These are usually generated by undersea earthquakes or volcanic eruptions that produce shock waves transmitted at very high velocities through the oceans. Surface waves are produced, but these are not normally very large when traveling through deep water. They become more massive and dangerous as they enter the shallower conditions around coastal regions, when the front of the wave is slowed and the rear of the wave catches up with it, creating a crest that can rise to 60 feet (20 m) or more. The Indian Ocean tsunami of December 26, 2004, was created by the shifting of the floor of the ocean to the west of Sumatra in Southeast Asia. The waves generated struck the neighboring coast of Sumatra with great force, flooding the low-lying lands and their settlements and destroying whole towns. The tsunami passed westward over the Indian Ocean, striking the island of Sri Lanka and the east coast of India, as well as the coast of Somalia on the east of Africa. The high density of populations along these coasts, especially in Southeast Asia, led to a very high level of human fatalities, undoubtedly exceeding 300,000 people.

the inland cities, such as Paris, Moscow, Chicago, and St. Louis, have rivers or lakes linking them to other parts of the country or to the open ocean. Coastal development involves certain risks, including storms and tidal waves or tsunamis (see the "Storms and tsunamis" sidebar on page 9), but there must have been a strong motive for settlements to develop close to the sea. Undoubtedly, this common feature is related to the importance of water as a means of transport, especially in historical times, before the days of air travel. Other cities rose to prominence because of their key position in relation to ancient overland trade routes, such as the Asian cities of Tehran, Tashkent, and Delhi. Communication, therefore, is one of the most important factors involved in the establishment and the growth of major urban settlements. But was this always so?

The very first urban settlements seem to have developed independently in several different parts of the world (see "The origin of towns and cities," pages 162–165), ranging from Mesoamerica (Mexico and surrounding areas) and Peru in the New World, to the Nile Valley, Lower Mesopotamia (modern Iraq), the Indus Valley (modern Pakistan), and northern China in the Old World. These ancient cities were situated in or near centers of agriculture, and their development in these locations was undoubtedly related to the production of surplus food, so that some of the workforce could develop specialist skills. So the first cities were indeed closely linked to agricultural production. But the expansion of agricultural areas and the spread of civilization generated the need to travel and trade between settlements, and it was then that communications became the most important feature in the success of a city.

The growing importance of communications in the world is well illustrated by the example of the Roman Empire, which once ruled the entire known world of its time. It was based upon one city, the so-called Eternal City of Rome. By 2,000 years ago, the armies of Rome had become the dominant force in what are now Europe, western Asia, and northern Africa. The city of Rome had begun its existence as a small grouping of huts during the Iron Age, perhaps around 2,700 years ago, supported by local agriculture in the fertile valley of the Tiber River. The river itself provided an effective transport link to the Mediterranean Sea and from there to most of the known world of that time. Conflict with neighboring villages and tribes led to Rome's expansion and domination of a region, so that by 509 B.C.E. it declared itself a republic and set out to conquer the rest of what is now Italy. Having achieved that, Rome used its strong position close to the sea to develop its imperialist ambitions and to extend its empire. In 202 B.C.E. the Romans destroyed Carthage (another coastal city but in northern Africa) and thus became undisputed masters of the Mediterranean. Having established this supremacy, Rome was able to absorb the produce of its conquered nations, taking in grain from Egypt and North Africa, minerals and semiprecious stones from northern Europe, and slaves from all of its empire. Rome's centrality and the ease of communications by sea therefore contributed to its success as a dominant city.

In the New World, New York was founded on the island of Manhattan, lying between two major rivers that provided access to the vast interior of North America. It also lay on the east coast of the continent, facing the trading nations of the Old World across the Atlantic. Its position, therefore, enabled it to become a major urban development supporting international trade and business. Its geographical position permitted New York to become established, and the city exploited its geographical advantages as it expanded and grew in importance.

Patterns of development

We have seen that there are patterns of agricultural and urban settlement that can be explained on the global scale by the demands of climate, soils, and (in the case of cities) communications with other areas. But when viewed at a landscape scale, the patterns of settlement become rather more complicated. Put yourself in the place of a group of prehistoric people (perhaps several families together with sheep, goats, possibly a few cattle, and some bags of grain) who enter a densely forested valley in a temperate region of the world. Where would you choose to settle? What would be the best sites for building dwellings, felling forest for grazing, or cultivating the land for growing cereal crops? Obviously, you would need to consider many factors. The crops might be the most demanding aspect of your plan, so you would need to look for deep, rich soils capable of supplying the growing plants with all their needs. The settlement would also have to be supplied with a source of water for drinking, washing, and possibly irrigation if the summer became hot and dry. A south-facing aspect would mean a longer growing season with a better chance of ripening the grain, but it could result in the risk of summer drought. You would also need to think about the task of forest clearance. The best soils would likely carry the heaviest crop of timber and so would be the most difficult to clear. Sites for grazing would be less of a problem, because grassland can be generated even on shallow and relatively dry soils. Consequently, people who concentrate on grazing animals might opt for clearing the ridges of the landscape, while arable farmers might clear the valleys. Sites for the development of homes would need a good water supply but should not be in danger of flooding. They would also need to be sheltered from adverse weather conditions, such as high winds, so they would be best situated in the valleys.

In particularly mountainous conditions, such as the Alpine country of Switzerland, the need for two types of farming, arable and pastoral, has led to a complex pattern of settlement. The main villages and the arable farming are in the valleys, but small settlements and huts are often situated high on the mountains near the timberline, and these are used by the pastoralists for summer dwellings. The cattle or sheep spend their summer on the high pastures, where they consume the rich growth of herbaceous vegetation, and then descend to the valleys in the fall and are housed in sheds through the severe winter weather. In their cattle sheds, the animals are fed hay that has been gathered from hay meadows, from which the animals have been excluded during the summer, or on the foliage of certain trees, such as ash and elm, which are stripped from the trees and dried to produce winter fodder. These varied patterns of land use result in a mosaic, or patchwork, landscape in which there are areas given to vegetable gardens, areas for hay meadows, patches of managed woodland for timber, other woodland that is stripped for fodder, open grassland with animals, and so on. Interspersed with this patchwork, there will be blocks of the original forest, which may be broken into different-size sections by the tracks and roadways that run though them, linking each village to the next. Movement of people with their flocks in the different seasons is called a *transhumance* system of pastoralism. It is common in the mountain regions of the world and was extensively used in the Sierra Nevada of California in the 19th century.

The type of landscape resulting is often referred to as a cultural landscape, in other words, a landscape that has been produced by the activities and management of human beings. Often these patterns of land use result in quite a high biodiversity, because many different habitats are present and a wealth of wildlife, meaning wild plants as well as animals, can be supported by them. But each type of habitat is present as a fragment, a small area isolated from similar habitats and surrounded by very different types of vegetation. Movement between fragments may not be a problem for mobile animals (or for plants with efficient dispersal systems) that are able and willing to cross alien territory in order to reach their destinations. But for organisms with poor dispersal mechanisms

Pastoral farming at Eisenhower Farm in Gettysburg, Pennsylvania. The patchwork of fields and hedges surrounded by forested hills results in a high degree of landscape diversity. (Courtesy of Fogstock)

or behavior patterns that prevent them from straying far from their home ranges, *fragmentation* of habitats can be a serious problem.

Landscape fragmentation can take place in a variety of ways. One habitat may retreat as another expands, such as when an area of grassland comes into contact with forest and the grassland can be expanded by felling more of the trees. This process is known as encroachment. Or new openings may be made deep within the forest, and then each may expand and eventually join together. For instance, a road may be constructed through the forest, thus dividing it into two halves. Logging or other activities may then take place along the sides of the road, reducing the area of forest on each side of the road. The original habitat (in this case, forest) thus becomes split into smaller and smaller fragments, each of which gradually becomes farther and farther separated from similar fragments. Animals and plants that require deep forest habitats and large areas in which to live and breed are the first to be eliminated in this situation. They may be unwilling to make the journey between the fragments, or they may risk being killed by predators during such crossings. As a consequence, they may become locally extinct.

One species facing this type of problem is the spotted owl, which lives in the forests of the western United States. This is a small owl that prefers old-growth forest rather than cleared and regrowth areas. As the western forests have been logged and split into smaller lots, the owl population has suffered a decrease in its numbers. One of the main problems the spotted owl faces is that it is likely to be attacked by larger predatory birds, such as northern goshawks or horned owls, while making the dangerous flight from one block of old forest to another. The risk of predation is greatest along the edges and in the gaps of the forest. A fragmented forest is particularly rich in gaps and edges, so further fragmentation and further loss of old-growth patches could put the survival of the spotted owl at risk. Unless the remaining old-growth forest is protected, populations of the owl will become scarcer and more scattered, until eventually it is liable to become completely extinct as a species.

In some respects, the fragments of habitats that can be found in the agricultural landscape are rather like islands in the ocean. They come in different sizes, and they are separated by different distances from one another. By developing this analogy, biogeographers have developed a series of rules that can generally be applied to fragmented habitats:

1. The larger the island or fragment, the more species it will contain. Large fragments are generally rich in species and smaller fragments increasingly poor.
2. The rate of extinction is greater in small islands. Small islands will have longer edges in relation to their area, so the chances of predation are greater, as in the case of the spotted owl.
3. The greater the distance between islands, the lower are the chances of an animal reestablishing itself if it should become extinct at a site. The immigration rate on a smaller island is lower because wandering organisms are less likely to chance upon it.
4. When a population of an organism is split into fragments, it is less likely to be wiped out by an epidemic disease. But there is a danger that the isolated patches will fail to link up to interbreed, and this can lead to isolated populations becoming genetically uniform.

There are exceptions to these rules. Some small habitat fragments can be very rich in species, perhaps as a result of unusual conditions or because of an unusual history. But the rules apply to most fragmented habitats, so the development of patchy landscapes can represent a threat to certain species, especially those that need large areas for living and breeding. On the other hand, as we shall see, such landscapes can offer great opportunities to those animals and plants that are able to cope with fragmentation.

Patterns within cities

Just as the general landscape is patterned, so is the layout of the city. In part, this can be explained by the fact that cities grow during the course of time. From an original settlement that may consist of no more than a few houses, villages and towns expand to become cities. As they expand, their nature changes, and the kinds of activities carried on in different districts alter. No two cities are exactly alike in their patterns,

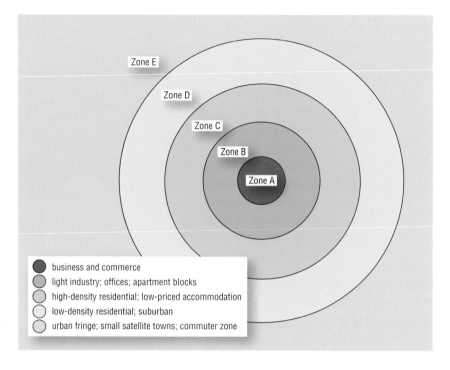

In general, the city can often be divided into a series of concentric zones, each with its own characteristic features and activities. Cities usually develop outward from the ancient center during the course of time, but the central regions are usually the commercial hearts of modern cities.

Zone E

Zone D

Zone C

Zone B

Zone A

- business and commerce
- light industry; offices; apartment blocks
- high-density residential; low-priced accommodation
- low-density residential; suburban
- urban fringe; small satellite towns; commuter zone

but often one can detect zones around the city center that can be found in many cities. Right in the very middle of a modern city we find the main business and commercial area (Zone A). Typically, this consists of a skyscraper section that has completely replaced the original settlement from the foundation of the city. Relatively few people will actually reside in this central district, so the main buildings are office blocks, together with department stores or shopping malls and places of entertainment, including theaters, concert halls, museums, and art galleries. There may also be large public parks and gardens in this central zone. Around the central development is often a zone of light industry (Zone B), scattered office buildings and apartment blocks that house many of the workers from the city center. The buildings of this zone are often older than those of the city center. Although money may be available for the frequent redevelopment of the center, there is usually less investment in replacing the buildings of this secondary zone, unless the city center needs to expand outward. The next zone (Zone C) often consists of high-density residences that house the lower-paid workers. Newly arrived immigrant workers often settle in this zone, where housing is relatively cheap and travel to a place of work is simple. Beyond this lies a zone (Zone D) of low-density housing in which higher-paid workers reside. This is the main residential suburban zone of the city and it is usually well supplied with arterial roads and rail networks permitting the residents easy access to the city center, where they usually commute daily to earn their money. Houses are often larger in this zone, with bigger gardens and more extensive recreational facilities, such as swimming pools, tennis courts, open parks, and so on.

Beyond the suburban residential zone, there is often a more diffuse and ill-defined zone (Zone E) from which some residents commute into the city. Often this consists of a series of smaller towns situated along radiating highways that give access to the city itself. These small towns may be intermingled with rural areas supporting small farms or areas of horticulture. Not all of the people in this commuter zone will need to travel to the city each day, because many will be

A city seen from the air. The tall buildings on the left form the commercial center of the city (Zone A), which is surrounded by zones of light industry and residential accommodation. (Courtesy of Fogstock)

employed in local service industries, shopping centers, garden supply industries, and recreation. So the city may be surrounded by a series of smaller satellite towns that feed the main city with workers and draw upon the wealth of the city (through the commuting workforce) for their sustenance. Many of our older and larger cities have expanded to engulf these satellite towns, and these have now become local centers within the larger mass of urban development.

The existence of zones within and around the city is reminiscent of many natural ecosystems. Take a pond, for instance. In the center there is deep water. The water is shallower around the edges and floating waterweeds manage to grow there. Even farther from the center, we usually find a zone of reeds and other emergent plants forming a marsh. On the landward side of this, trees such as alders create a wet woodland habitat. This concentric arrangement of different habitats around a pond forms a system of zonation that is commonly found in nature. The city displays just the same kind of zonation, but there is one major difference. In the case of ponds, the new development comes from the edges as the reeds invade the center and cause it to become silted and shallower. The outer vegetation will eventually come to dominate the whole region as wetland trees follow the reeds and invade the central regions. In the city the development comes from the center and expands outward, swallowing up the surrounding countryside in urban development.

Within each of the zones of a city, one can discern an even more complicated pattern of habitats. Just as the agricultural landscape can be regarded as a mosaic of habitat fragments, so, too, can the zones of the city. This is most obvious when you fly over a city and can observe how the blocks of concrete that form the offices and dwellings are separated by road systems that, in turn, may carry trees and strips of grass along their edges. Gardens can occur even in the center of cities, perhaps even on rooftops, forming patches of green. They often become larger and more frequent as we move out into the suburbs and may be linked together in extended strips. Parks are also found in most cities, forming larger islands of vegetation within a sea of sterile brick. Aquatic habitats may also be present. The rivers or docklands that have historically provided a means of communication to a city have often become important wildlife habitats within the city and may act as a means of communication for the wildlife, too, providing them with corridors along which they can move from one wetland site to another. Small lakes and ponds in the city parks add to the mosaic of habitat patches in the city.

Do these patches, like those habitat fragments in the rural countryside, also obey the rules of island biogeography? Generally speaking, the answer seems to be yes. Larger lakes usually support more species of ducks than small ones. Also, if you check vacant lots for invasive plants, you will find more species on the larger lots. It is also true that short distances between such habitat patches lead to faster invasion and richer habitats. The lesson here for conservation in the city is that a diversity of habitats will support a diversity of plant and animal wildlife, but the larger the habitat patches and the closer they are together, the greater that diversity will be. We shall return to this subject in chapter 6.

The microclimate of cities

Although climate is often an important factor in determining what plants and animals can survive in a particular region, there are always locations where an organism can escape from the most severe effects of climate, and the more sensitive plants and animals do just that. On the forest floor, sunshine is not as intense as in the open during the day, and neither does it become so cold at night. The wind speed is lower in such a sheltered locality, and the undisturbed air builds up higher levels of humidity. So plants that are easily desiccated, or are sensitive to heat or to frost, may escape the effects of a severe climate if they grow on the forest floor. Invertebrate animals, such as insects and worms, may go further to escape extreme conditions and live within rotting logs, beneath stones, or underground, where the climatic conditions are even less variable. The type of climate found at this small scale is called the *microclimate*.

Even large animals may seek out locations with favorable microclimates. A lizard may bask in the sun on top of a stone wall. Since it is unable to generate its own body heat in the way that mammals do, it needs to seek energy from the Sun to keep its body temperature high enough to sustain its activity. A mountain lion may do the reverse and seek the cool of a cave during the hot day, avoiding the problem of overheating. Each is seeking a particular microclimate that serves its purpose. In the course of their evolution, human beings have behaved in precisely the same way. Cave-dwelling cultures were looking for a microclimate that was dry and warm in winter (especially when heated by a fire) and cool in summer. But caves were not sufficiently abundant to serve a growing population, and they were not present in all the regions that humans wished to occupy. The answer was to build artificial caves, or shelters, using whatever raw materials were available. Vegetation is one obvious answer, so branches of trees provided a basis for the construction of primitive dwellings. Humans were not the first animals to hit upon this idea, however. Birds had long been building nests, including ones for roosting rather than breeding, and some of these can have elaborate constructions with roof canopies to protect them from sun and rain. Many primates also build such nests, as do invertebrates like ants and termites. All of these animals are seeking to modify their own microclimate to suit their own needs.

Humans have the advantage of a high brain capacity and the ability to innovate in their constructions of dwellings, depending on the local circumstances. Where wood was not available, mud bricks could be made and built into complex structures. If caves were not available, then artificial caves could be constructed using stones or turf cut from the soil. In the frozen north, ice blocks were an alternative; although the material may not sound very attractive for house construction, the insulating properties of ice do allow the inhabitant to build up the temperature inside the ice dwelling. On the Ice Age plains of Siberia, where raw materials were in particularly short supply, the Stone Age mammoth hunters even used the bones of the mammoths in the building of their huts. It was this kind of intelligence and adaptability that allowed people to spread into even the most inhospitable regions of the world, where they survived by building their own microclimate around themselves.

What about modern cities? If an igloo or a bone hut can alter the local microclimate, the ability of a city such as Los Angeles or New York to do so must be even greater. The huge scale of our modern buildings does indeed create a very complicated city microclimate. The city microclimate is made even more distinct from the local climate because we generate so much heat in our cities. In an igloo the main source of warmth is the radiated body heat of the inhabitants. In a modern house we inject energy that is derived from other sources, such as fossil fuels (gas or oil) or electricity generated from these materials, or perhaps derived from renewable energy resources such as hydroelectric generators or wind farms. In some cases we take energy directly from the Sun and heat our homes by solar energy. Then, when things get hot in summer, we may use the same energy resources to cool our houses by air-conditioning.

As well as the space heating within our city dwellings and offices, we also generate heat as we travel around in our various means of transport. The internal combustion engines that drive most of our cars and buses burn fossil fuels and generate a great deal of waste heat that is forced out into the atmosphere in the exhaust fumes. This raises the temperature of our city streets, as do the streetlights that we keep switched on in the city throughout the night. Industrial cities have factories that also lose waste heat to their surroundings.

The outcome is that cities are almost always warmer than surrounding regions, averaging about 1 to 3°F (0.5 to 1.5°C) over a year and often by around 9°F (5°C) or more on some days. Cities, therefore, have their own microclimates, and the animals and plants that inhabit them often reflect these distinctive microclimates (see "Opportunities in the city," pages 126–130). The fact that rose-ringed parakeets (originally inhabitants of India and subsequently escaped from captivity in many other parts of the world) can now establish breeding colonies in cities as far north as New York and London clearly illustrates how the microclimate of a city can override the surrounding general climate as far as its inhabitants (both human and wildlife) are concerned. Cities can be regarded as "heat islands" lying within a generally cooler sea of surrounding countryside.

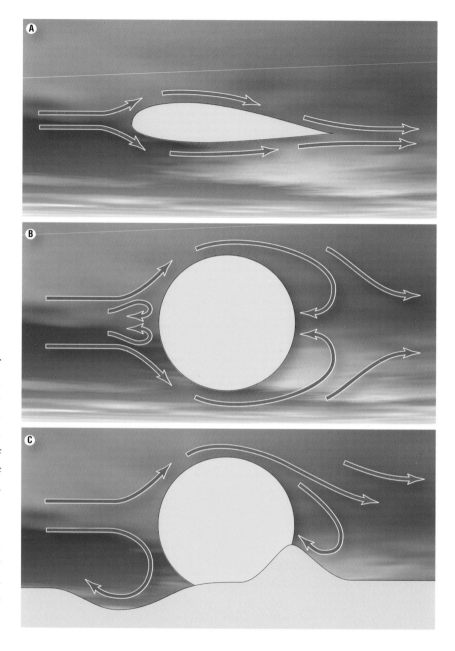

Airflow patterns over different objects. (A) A streamlined object, such as the wing of an aircraft, causes a minimum deflection of the wind. (B) A "bluff body" disrupts airflow and thus creates eddies of circulating air. (C) A bluff body lying on the surface of the ground creates eddies that may cause erosion and deposition of mobile soil.

The heat island effect in cities results not only from the heat generated where people gather together, but also from the way in which our buildings have created windbreaks and complicated patterns of light and shade over the landscape. If you have ever sat on a sandy beach and looked at the small piles of windblown sand that accumulate around any object, such as a shell or a pebble or a blade of grass, you will be aware that even a small object modifies the pattern of air movement over the surface of the ground. The figure on page 22 shows how this principle operates. Any obstruction to airflow deflects the air to either side; the separated air masses then join again behind the body. If the shape of the obstacle is smooth and aerodynamic the disruption to airflow is minimal. This is the type of flow observed around a falcon's wing, giving it minimum air resistance and maximum speed, and it is the aim of aircraft, rocket, and automobile designers to mimic this type of aerodynamic structure. In contrast, an object lacking aerodynamic shape, known to physicists as a *bluff body,* creates a much more complicated pattern of airflow (see the figure on page 22). The point immediately in front of the body, where the airflow separates to pass either side, will have a very low speed of wind movement; air is effectively blocked by the obstruction. There may even be some bouncing back of air, resulting in a small volume where the air movement is reversed. Behind the object, there is another region where airflow is severely slowed or reversed. Small areas of swirling air called *eddies* are produced.

Returning to the pebble on a sandy beach, we can see how these patterns of airflow have resulted in the complexity of sand deposition around the pebble. Where the air has first met with the obstruction, there may be a slight hollow in the sand, undermining the pebble, caused by the reversal of airflow at this point. Behind the pebble, the slowing of the air causes the sand that is carried by the wind to settle out of suspension, because slower-moving air cannot hold the larger grains of sand. So a small pile, or dune, of sand develops on the sheltered side of the stone, called the *lee.* Sometimes you may find a similar small pile in front of the stone, depending on whether the conditions in front of the obstruction produce still air or a reverse flow.

If a pebble on a beach can create such complex wind patterns, it is clear that a series of buildings arranged close together will result in even more disturbance to airflow. Factors such as the height of a building, the distance between buildings, and the orientation of streets in relation to the prevailing wind will all influence the pattern that develops. Tall buildings arranged close together in a street at right angles to the prevailing air-flow will create eddies that are limited to the upper layers only and may not be felt on the streets below, where the air can remain relatively still. Wider spaces between buildings or lower height of the buildings allows the eddies to descend closer to the ground level. If the street is oriented in the same direction as the wind, then a tunnel effect is produced and the wind will funnel along the street, enclosed by buildings on either side. In practice, of course, winds vary in direction and speed, so all cities are occasionally subject to these wind-tunnel effects, Chicago being a proverbial example. Thus the city street behaves almost like a canyon. City wildlife responds according-ly to this similarity. The patterns of wind movement and tur-bulence in cities are also important when we consider the dis-persal of pollutants, particularly those emitted by vehicles on the streets. A lack of air turbulence at street level can result in the buildup of gaseous emissions and small particles at ground level, for they are not being dispersed by air movements.

City microclimates involve other factors in addition to air movements. Sunlight itself is absorbed by and reflected from the surfaces of buildings. In physics the amount of light reflected from a surface is termed its *albedo*. A white surface has a high albedo, while a dark surface has a low albedo. The color of building materials thus affects the heat absorbance and reflection in a city street. In general, light-colored mate-rials reflect the light and so tend to be cooler; this is why low-latitude cities so often have white-walled buildings. But if the streets are wide, this could have the effect of reflecting sun-light down to the ground, resulting in a heat buildup at street level. Narrow streets and white walls are the simple answer to this problem, and the characteristic arrangement of buildings in old cities in hot regions, such as Seville in Spain, has been

---

(opposite page) *(A) Airflow patterns within a city, showing the eddies created within the streets by high buildings. (B) The pattern of solar energy distribution in a city. Energy may be received directly from the Sun or reflected from the sides of buildings, while some locations remain in permanent shade.*

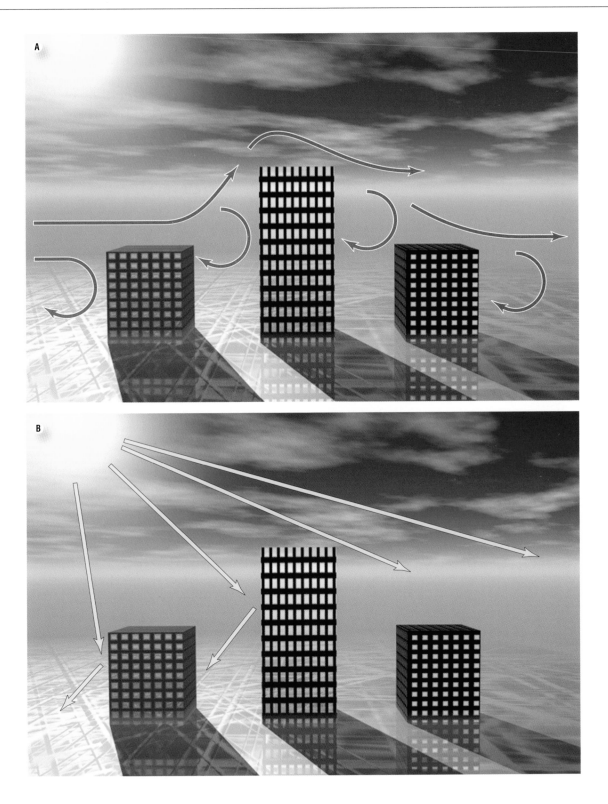

developed on this plan. Narrow streets likewise permit less sunlight to penetrate directly to ground level, again having a cooling influence. Narrow streets can also affect humidity, the dark, still air at ground level retaining higher water contents. Even the pattern of precipitation is affected by the presence of buildings, more rain impacting on the windward side of the structure and draining down to the ground from its walls. Exposed parts of a city therefore receive more rainfall than protected sites in the lee of buildings.

The microclimate of agricultural regions

Just as cities create their own microclimates, so do areas of agriculture. As discussed earlier, the development of agriculture in a region usually involves the modification of the original (often quite uniform) vegetation and the construction of a new surface cover to the land, frequently arranged in a patchwork, or mosaic, fashion (see "Patterns of development," pages 11–15). The change from a uniform structure to an irregular or heterogeneous surface results in a modified microclimate, whose character depends on the nature and the scale of the patchwork of the new landscape. The opening of a forest cover to produce clearings, for example, results in complicated patterns of air movements, similar to those found in cities but generally on a smaller scale. Wind speeds are greatly reduced in forest patches, but some penetration takes place, especially below the canopy, in what can be called the trunk space. The rate of air movement in the trunk space is generally only 10 to 20 percent of that above the canopy, depending on the nature of the forest structure.

Downwind of the forest there is an area of eddies and generally slower wind speed, but speed picks up the farther one moves from the forest edge. Just how far this protective wind

---

(opposite page) *(A) Airflow patterns in the countryside, showing the deflection of the wind by hedges and patches of woodland. (B) The pattern of incident solar energy in a country landscape. Openings within a woodland canopy may receive direct sunlight and be sheltered from the wind, resulting in local heat accumulation.*

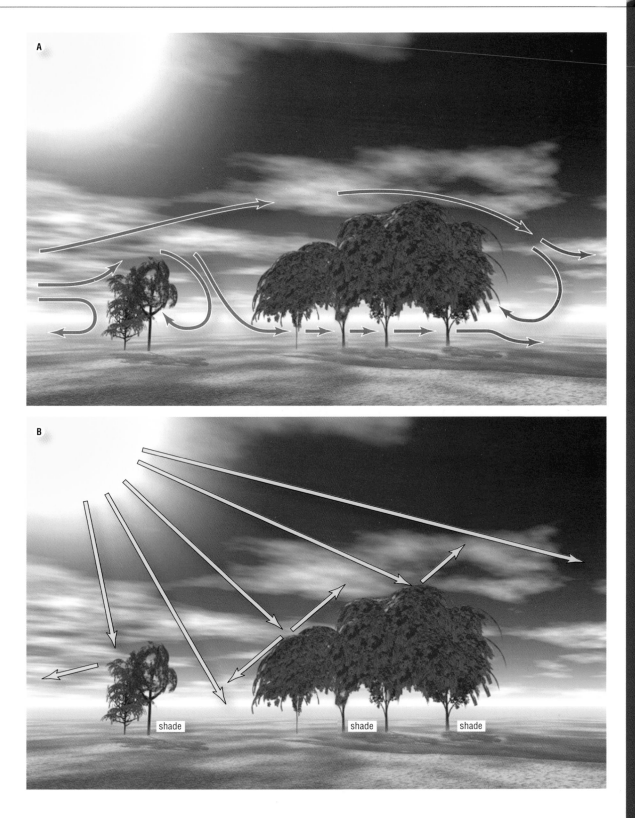

A

B

shade

shade

shade

The deposition of salt carried by the wind onto a tree close to the ocean. Figures show the percentage of solid salt arriving at different parts of the tree. Salt deposition on the exposed upper part of the tree may be sufficient to kill its growing points, deforming its pattern of growth.

shadow stretches depends on the height of the trees, but the wind speed at ground level is usually reduced downwind for a distance of about five or six times the height of the trees. So, patches of forest in an area of arable agriculture have an important effect, lowering wind speeds and protecting plowed soils from wind erosion. Large areas of open soils are much more susceptible to the effect of winds, including the drying influence of the moving air. Wide, open fields may be easier and cheaper to manage for the farmer, but they can produce a "dust bowl" effect, resulting in soil erosion.

Even a hedge around a field can have a strong influence on wind speeds. Such windbreaks can also act as traps for mobile soils, just like grasses on a sand dune. Particles suspended in the air strike the windward side of the hedge and become trapped there. If such particles are carried over the hedge, then the lower wind speed in the eddies behind the hedge can lead to their becoming deposited on the sheltered lee side. An example that shows just how effective a filter a hedge can be is shown in the figure on this page. In this example, a hedge close to the ocean has been analyzed to check how much of the airborne salt-rich particles and rainfall being blown from the sea has accumulated on the leaves and twigs. The figures are expressed as percentages of the total salt load that is deposited on the hedge each day. It can be seen that the side of the hedge facing the sea has a much heavier load of salt than the lee side, which is protected from the wind. About 80 percent of salt deposition occurs on the windward side, a fact that shows how effectively the hedge is acting as a filter.

In pastoral systems the height of the vegetation has a considerable influence on the microclimate near the ground. Tall grasses act rather like small forests; they reduce light penetration and wind speed so that the climate at the soil surface has lower light intensity, is more stable in its temperature, and is more humid than the air above the canopy. These conditions are generally favorable to the invertebrate animals that live there, many of which are sensitive to desiccation. Short grassland, on the other hand, offers less protection for small animals at the soil surface. There is more wind and light penetration through the grass canopy, so during sunny days the humidity falls and the temperature rises. Similarly, at night the temperature falls and frost may even penetrate.

A grain field has a relatively uniform microclimate. Only the breaks in the canopy interrupt the flow of air over the surface of the crop. (Courtesy of Fogstock)

In the case of arable crops, surface conditions may change considerably during the course of a year. Soils are usually plowed to prepare for the planting of the crop, and open soils have no protection from sun, wind, and rain. The albedo (reflectivity) of bare soils is generally low because the dark color absorbs solar energy and becomes heated. Once the crop begins to grow, the complexity of the architecture of leaves and stems increases, and the soil surface becomes more fully protected. Albedo increases, especially if the crop is an annual crop, like wheat, that dries to a pale color as the grain ripens. Finally, with the harvesting of the crop, the soil is exposed to the elements once again and the cycle is complete.

From these examples, it can be seen that the agricultural landscape has a complex microclimate that varies through the course of the seasons. In general it can be said that the climatic impact of humans, in disturbing the original ecosystems and establishing farmland or cities, imposes mosaic patterns with varied microclimates. Perhaps this is the reason why high population density of people is often associated with high species diversity. We actually diversify our environment. On the other hand, one can see that a very high density of people, or very intensive land use in agriculture, is likely to result in increasing uniformity of either city or farmland, which can only serve to lower the diversity of wildlife. Clearly there is a delicate balance to be struck.

Conclusions

Geography plays a key role in determining where farms and cities have become established. Agricultural lands are found only where the climate permits crops to grow or domesticated animals to survive and graze. Very cold and very dry parts of the world are not suitable for agriculture. The very high latitudes (the polar regions), besides being cold, also have the disadvantage of short winter days or even darkness, so that the growing season is very limited. Cities, on the other hand, are generally situated where communications are good rather than where agricultural productivity is highest. Historically, travel by boat or by pack animal was the most effective

means of movement, so cities are often located around oceans, on rivers, or on overland trade routes.

Both farms and cities change the topography, and consequently the biodiversity, of the location they occupy. The development of agriculture over the world has caused great changes in the landscape, the most important of which is the fragmentation of the original vegetation cover. Farmland is a mosaic of land patches. Some species of wildlife have been lost as a consequence, especially as the patches of native vegetation have become smaller and more widely scattered. But the creation of diversity in the landscape has encouraged other species, and consequently the overall range of species in farmland can be surprisingly high. Cities are very artificial landscapes that are designed primarily for human habitation and use, but they have an ecology of their own. Distinct

The city of Rome, Italy, lies upon the banks of the Tiber River. The presence of a river within the heart of a city greatly increases its variety of habitats and biodiversity. (Courtesy of Peter D. Moore)

zones exist in the cities where different activities (such as financial, retail, manufacturing, residential, and recreation) take place. Some of these zones provide a diverse array of opportunities for adaptable animals and plants to survive and even thrive.

Finally, farmland and cities affect their local climate, known as the microclimate. The concrete structures of the city and the hedges, woodland, and arable crops of the agricultural areas all have an impact on the movement of air in their vicinity. Light penetration, temperature variation, and the humidity of the air are all affected by the development of the cities that house us and the fields that supply our food. These, in turn, affect the lives of the creatures that share our habitats.

CHAPTER 2

GEOLOGY OF FARMS AND CITIES

Geology forms the basis of every ecosystem. The rocks that underlie the land surface of the Earth have a major effect upon the landscape and upon the soils that form in any particular region. These in turn have an impact on where rivers run, what kinds of vegetation can develop, what raw materials are available to humans, and what kind of crops can grow in the area. So geology can be regarded as the physical setting against which the story of human settlement and history has unfolded. Like the backdrop in the stage production of a play, it has a strong influence upon all that takes place.

Landscape

The term *landscape* is likely to bring to mind the physical form of a region, the hills and valleys, the rivers and plains. This can be called the *topography* of the geographical setting. Topography, the shape and form of a landscape, is affected by many factors, such as past climate, tectonic activity (including earthquakes, volcanic eruptions, and the like), the length of time over which the region has evolved, and the solid geology that underlies it. Rocks come in many different forms, but most important from a landscape point of view is how hard they are and how porous they are to water. Among the hardest of rocks is granite. Formed by the crystallization of magma (the molten material that underlies the Earth's crust) as it is brought to the surface in volcanoes, this rock is typically formed when continents collide. Its texture varies according to how quickly its components have crystallized, but fine-grained granite is not easily eroded by water or ground away by glacier ice, so it often produces impressive scenery of mountains and cliffs. Yosemite Valley in California is one of the most impressive areas of granite scenery on Earth.

33

Limestone is a sedimentary rock, formed slowly by the accumulation of deposits from former living organisms that existed in ancient shallow, warm seas. The rock is not very hard and is porous to water movement. It is soluble but, because of its porosity, it often produces a landscape rich in rugged cliffs and peaks, with caves and potholes that have been left behind as the water has sunk into the ground. Sandstone may also produce hilly country because water passes through the porous material rather than running over its surfaces, so the process of erosion is relatively slow. Clay, on the other hand, is not porous, but it is soft, so when water runs over it the result is often erosion. Where clays are found among other rocks in a landscape, it is often the clays that are most eroded, and therefore the lowest-lying. It is these valley clays that support the rivers and wetlands.

In determining the nature of the landscape, geology thus has a profound influence on the available setting for the development of human settlements. The landscape affects the vegetation, the soils, and even the climate of a particular location. It affects the nature of communications with other areas, and it also determines what materials are available for the construction of dwellings or other buildings in a developing city. Geology may also determine the availability of the resources that are needed for industrial or other purposes.

Geology and the city

Early cities were usually located either in places that were easy to defend from enemies, such as on hilltops, or in places that provided good communications with other areas, often close to the sea or in river valleys, where transporting people and commodities was often easier in ancient times (see "From village to town and city," pages 166–171). The cities situated in river valleys and floodplains are often based upon clay. Those in coastal regions are more varied in their geology. Most existing cities were founded in days when transport was much more difficult than in current times, so many of the factors that led to their geological location may no longer be so relevant. Indeed, some ancient cities are no longer as important as they formerly were because of the changing nature of trade and transport.

In the Middle East, which was a center of early civilization and urbanization (the development of cities), many of the early settlements, some more than 7,000 years old, were located in the valleys of large rivers, such as the Tigris and the Euphrates. Trade routes, by land and water, passed through the region and the cities grew as trading centers. Situated in the river valleys of Mesopotamia, these cities were not easily defended from attack, and their histories reflect this fact. They passed through the hands of various conquering nations. The cities' location in the extensive floodplains of the rivers also meant that the main building material was dried mud, so dwellings and walls were constructed from mud brick. Using these bricks, however, the ancient Mesopotamians were still able to build very large structures, 60 feet (18 m) or more high. The mud brick walls were quite strong but were troublesome in the rainy season, when they became saturated with water and were liable to swell and burst the walls. To overcome this, the walls were supplied with small holes, called weeper holes, through which excess water could drain away. Both the construction of high walls and the elevation of the settlements within these walls provided a degree of defensive capability even on the flat plains of the river valleys. Some of these buildings, called ziggurats, have survived intact to the present day, which indicates their strength and durability.

Due to the importance of river valleys for communication, as well as their agricultural productivity, several of the great early civilizations were based in such locations. Egypt is an obvious example. The delta of the Nile River was extremely rich agricultural land, which flooded annually as the rains of East Africa caused the swollen river to burst its banks and bring fresh nutrients to the surrounding soils. The mud produced in these floods also provided the raw material for brick manufacture so, as in the case of the Mesopotamian cities, mud brick was the basic geological material available for building. Reeds growing along the banks of the Nile and in the delta marshes provided additional building materials, either in the form of thatch for roofs or as a reinforcing agent within the bricks themselves. Defense was less of a problem here because the cities of the Nile Valley were protected by great expanses of desert. Bringing an army across such terrain was very difficult, and Egypt was able to develop in relative peace and isolation with little fear of attack, although some enemies managed to overcome the geographical difficulties and conquer this isolated nation. As in Mesopotamia, the large buildings and palaces of Egypt were constructed from mud bricks. Timber was also imported from the Mediterranean lands and some may even have been grown locally in the delta. Hard rock, such as limestone, was available from the coast and surrounding areas, but this material was reserved for special purposes, such as carving statues, which indicates its value. Even more precious was the igneous (volcanic) basalt from Upper Egypt in the south, which must have been difficult to transport by water and was reserved for the use of the very top level of society.

The pyramids of Lower Egypt were built in stone. Not only was their construction an extraordinary feat of engineering, but also the collection of the raw materials must have involved a remarkable degree of effort. Generally, the central burial chamber was constructed of granite slabs, and then the outer mass of the pyramid was built of layers of limestone blocks. The granite slabs for the Great Pyramid of Cheops at Giza weighed around 50 tons each. The limestone blocks that were used to construct the outer part were between two and 15 tons each, and 2.3 million of these were used in the erection of the pyramid. By the time this pyramid was built (around 4,600 to 4,700 years ago), the civilization of the Lower Nile had shown itself capable of moving massive quantities of building materials over considerable distances in order to enhance the quality of their buildings.

At around the time when the Great Pyramid of Cheops was being constructed in Egypt, the Chinese civilization was germinating in eastern Asia. This was another river-based civilization, in which the farming peoples of the area used the Huang He (Yellow River) for transport. They built boats of timber and of bamboo for their communications up and down the river. Walled cities, constructed of local stone, were built along the banks of the rivers, and the entire civilization, with its communications leading eastward via the river to the Yellow Sea and the Pacific Ocean, was isolated from the developing nations of western Asia and southeast Europe.

Equally remote from these centers of civilization and development were the peoples of Central and South America, who were also developing agriculture and beginning the process of social living in cities. In the valleys, once more, adobe mud bricks formed the basic building material, even for ceremonial buildings such as the pyramids. But in the highlands of what is now Peru, settlements were built upon hilltops and stone was available as a building material. Massive stone buildings and complex architectural structures were built in the Andes during the height of the Peruvian civilization in the first millennium B.C.E.

In recent times the influence of local geology on the building materials available for cities has been less marked, especially in the last century or so, when artificial building materials have largely replaced natural ones. But we do not need to go very much further back into history to see the influence of local geology. Many of the towns and cities of Europe that date from 200 or more years ago have buildings dominated by local stone. Edinburgh and Aberdeen in Scotland, for example, are characterized by dark granite stones that have a strong impact on the visitor. Where wood is more abundant and more easily worked than stone, as in the old settlements of New England, then it provides a satisfactory alternative, though not so long lasting.

Most of the cities of North America have developed within the last 200 years and their buildings have been constructed with brick and concrete rather than natural stone. Bricks are made from clay or shale and are placed in an oven and baked before use. Modern bricks are smaller as well as harder than the old adobe mud bricks. Their hardness ensures that they will survive through rain and frost, and their small size has been adopted because it is so much easier for a builder to handle them. Recently, however, machinery for building has become more efficient and can deal with larger building blocks than are practicable when the bricks are laid by hand. The large building blocks of modern constructions are often made of concrete instead of the baked clay of former times. Concrete is a kind of artificial rock, made out of stone that has been ground and crushed, together with sand, water, and a binding agent, usually cement (derived from limestone). It is not really a modern invention; it was used by the Romans in the building of their aqueducts and amphitheaters. The Romans used slaves to handle large concrete blocks, but with the development of lifting machinery and cranes we can now build from concrete without using slaves. It is now possible to cast concrete into large slabs and to raise them into position using cranes so that the construction of large buildings can proceed very rapidly. This movement away from the use of local rocks in building has led to cities around the world becoming more uniform in their design and their construction materials. It has also allowed cities to develop even in the absence of appropriate local stone.

Before the development of modern building methods, however, the rocks that underlay cities affected the nature of the buildings that could be constructed. In the early Mesopotamian cities and in those of Central America, for example, tectonic activity brought a danger of earthquakes, and this influenced methods of construction, just as it does today in cities such as Los Angeles and San Francisco in California. The nature of the underlying rock also affects the height of buildings. Settlements in the deserts of Iran rarely have buildings above two stories in height, partly because of the instability of the sands upon which they are often built, and also because of the ever-present threat of earthquake. In New York it proved possible to construct extremely high buildings even 100 years ago, while in London, built on clay, the development of tall buildings has not been possible until relatively recently with the arrival of new construction methods and materials.

Some cities have arisen in locations where the geology has provided specific minerals or materials that are in demand. The Industrial Revolution, for example, led to the founding and the expansion of many cities close to the vital energy resource of coal. Smelting iron requires a great deal of energy to separate the metal from its parent rock. In prehistoric times this would have been supplied by wood burning, but the temperatures required are difficult to achieve in this way. Coal-burning furnaces revolutionized iron extraction, and the primitive methods used in Roman and medieval times were quickly replaced. Settlements close to coal deposits thrived under these conditions, so new cities developed in response to the geological conditions of an area. The other raw materials needed for iron extraction, iron ore and also limestone, were used in the process of smelting within a blast furnace. Sites where all three of these commodities were present were rare, and this gave rise to a need for easy transportation of one or another of the raw materials. The need for transport gave a great boost to the development of artificial waterways (canals) and the railways as a cheap and easy way of carrying heavy and bulky materials to the developing industrial cities. The revolution in transport over the past 200 years or so has meant that the old constraints on where cities might develop have been overcome. New cities can be linked by road, rail, and air connections, so urban developments are now set free from their early geological restrictions.

Geography and geology have strongly affected both the location and the building materials available in the founding of cities. All cities, however, are limited in their population growth by food supply, and the ability of surrounding areas (hinterland) to support cities in this way has often proved vital to the success of a city. Farms and cities are closely connected; without the farms the cities cannot survive. The influence of geology on agriculture is therefore an important consideration in determining the pattern of human settlement on the face of the Earth.

Geology and soils

Soils form a thin skin on the surface of the land and are a kind of boundary layer between the solid geology of the rocks and the atmosphere above. In fact, they are a mixture of both materials. Rocks break up into small fragments as a result of a process called *weathering*, and between these fragments the air of the atmosphere and water from precipitation are able to penetrate the soil. Soil, therefore, consists of a mixture of mineral particles, atmosphere, and water, together with the living things that occupy the mixture and the dead remains that they produce. Most plants grow in contact with the soil, usually with roots that delve into the complex underground structure in order to gain a supply of water and chemical elements. Different plants have varied requirements of the soil, and domesticated plants are no exception. The development of arable agriculture is therefore very dependent on the type of soil available in any area. Soil, along with climate, is one of the most important determinants of what kind of agriculture can be developed at any given location. In order to understand the agricultural ecosystem we need to consider in detail the nature of the formation and development of soils. The chemistry of the environment determines many of the processes that are carried out in ecosystems, and this certainly applies to agriculture.

Rocks vary greatly in their chemical constitution and in their physical hardness, but all rocks break down when they are exposed to the air and to the climatic conditions that they encounter near the surface. Rocks decompose in two distinct ways: by mechanical or physical processes, and by chemical reactions. Mechanical weathering involves the physical breakdown of rocks into smaller particles, and this can be brought about in a number of ways. Rocks are not uniform in their structure; they often consist of different materials mixed together, and these different materials may expand and contract at different rates when they are subjected to heat or to cold. When a rock is buried deep in a geological formation, it lies in a uniform set of conditions and there is very little variation in temperature. When it is brought to the surface by earth movements or by erosion, however, it begins to experience these temperature changes. Differential expansion and contraction of the various rock components effectively loosens them and opens up hairline fractures in the rock. Water, seeping through the rock, can then enter these crevices. When water freezes it expands, a fact well known to anyone who has had a water pipe burst during freezing weather. The force exerted by the expanding ice is quite sufficient to rupture metal pipes and it can equally well split rocks. Plant roots can also contribute to the mechanical weathering process. The fine roots of plants that penetrate the soil in search of water and chemical elements may look fragile and delicate, but they can also exert very considerable forces. As they slip into the fine cracks caused by frost action, they grow and expand, forcing apart the particles of rock and splitting them further.

The second type of weathering, chemical weathering, occurs when chemical reactions take place among the split fragments. Water itself is a remarkable compound that has the capacity to dissolve a wide range of substances. Soil weathering takes place over long timescales (many thousands of years), and in that time water is able to remove many different compounds in solution. The water that permeates soil is not pure. Even before landing on the soil surface, rainwater has already been able to dissolve certain materials from the atmosphere. Some of the gases in the atmosphere are soluble, such as carbon dioxide, sulfur dioxide, and the oxides of nitrogen. Carbon dioxide is a natural and universal component of the atmosphere that is present in quite low concentrations (usually below 0.04 percent). When it dissolves in water it forms carbonic acid, a weak acid but one that attacks some of the components of rock and renders them soluble. Carbonic acid can extract elements such as calcium, magnesium, and potassium from rock and form carbonates in the soil, where they are available for uptake by plant roots. The oxides of sulfur and nitrogen that exist in the atmosphere can be produced by volcanic activity but are increasingly found as a result of human pollution, especially by the burning of fossil fuels. These oxides also dissolve in water to form sulfuric and nitric acids, both of which are strong acids that can have a great impact on soil weathering. Under their influence, elements such as iron and aluminum become increasingly soluble. These metals can be toxic to plants, so the intense weathering that takes place under conditions of highly polluted acid rain can be harmful to both natural vegetation and crops.

One other form of chemical weathering occurs because of the presence of decaying organic matter in the soil. The dead remains of roots, leaves, animal corpses, fungi, and bacteria in the soil are broken down by the decomposers in the ecosystem. The first organisms to take advantage of dead material in the soil are the *detritivores*. These are invertebrate animals, ranging from earthworms to burying beetles and springtails, that ingest the dead material, extract some of the energy from it, and then cast out what remains in their feces. They play an important part in fragmenting the dead material, exposing greater surface areas to the further activity of fungi and bacteria. There are many different species of fungi and bacteria, each with its own specialist mode of nutrition. Some may concentrate their activities on the easily assimilated products of organic matter breakdown, such as sugars or amino acids (from proteins), while others specialize in larger and more complicated molecules, such as cellulose or lignin (from wood). Some of the breakdown products are themselves acidic in nature. Fats, for example, decompose into fatty acids, and lignin can produce polyuronic acids that contribute to the chemical weathering of the mineral soil particles. The decomposition of organic matter in the soil is thus an incremental process.

The weathering of rocks can produce a broad range of soil types, simply because the constitution of the rocks themselves is so variable. There are many types of granite, for example. The simplest type of granite consists of three types of minerals: feldspar, mica, and quartz. These three components crystallize separately from magma as it cools into granite, and physical weathering of granite can result in their release into the soil. One of the elements found in feldspar is potassium, and chemical weathering by rainwater releases this element in the form of a carbonate, which may then be absorbed by a plant root. After the potassium is removed from feldspar, the remaining material consists of kaolinite, one of a class of materials known as clay minerals. Kaolinite is also known as china clay and can be used in the ceramics industry. Mica breaks down to form potassium and magnesium carbonates, along with oxides of iron and aluminum. The quartz, however, is a simple and relatively inert compound, silicon dioxide, commonly known as sand. This material is unlikely to be degraded any further and remains in the soil, giving it a permanent mineral skeleton.

Other rocks produce different types of products. Sandstone consists largely of sand grains compacted together, so they will degrade physically but will remain little altered chemically. Limestone, on the other hand, consists largely of calcium carbonate. Although this is not very soluble in water, over long periods of exposure to the dilute acid of rainfall, limestone will dissolve completely. This means that limestone soils have no mineral skeleton at all, beyond the calcium carbonate fragments within it that are slowly dissolving. Limestone soils, therefore, are often very shallow and consist of a mixture of organic material with particles of calcium carbonate mixed in. Limestone is a sedimentary rock, which means that it was deposited from ancient oceans as particles fell to the bottom of the sea and accumulated there. In the case of limestone, the particles consist of calcium carbonate (lime) that has been extracted from the water by microscopic organisms and used in their shells. When these die, their shells join the sediments in the depths. Other sedimentary rocks, such as shale and sandstone, are derived from the recycling of particles eroded from the land. These have been washed into the oceans, where they sediment as weathered particles and become buried beneath huge pressures of accumulating sediments above them. When the compacted sediments are raised again by tectonic activity, they become exposed to the elements for a second (or more) time. The fact that some sedimentary rocks have had their components recycled means that they have already lost many of their soluble elements, so they are poorer and are far more uniform than the freshly produced rocks, such as those created by volcanic activity. Sedimentary rocks also differ in the particle sizes produced by weathering. Shales weather to produce mainly clay, resulting in poorly drained soils, while sandstones weather into sandy and freely drained soils.

Soil conditions and plant growth

It is evident that different rocks produce soils with varied composition, but how does this impact on plant growth, and in particular on crops? To be able to answer this question, we need to consider precisely what the plant needs from the soil.

The plant organ that is in closest contact with the soil is usually the root. Some plants have underground storage organs, such as stem tubers (for example, potatoes) and bulbs (for example, onions), but for most plants it is the root that conducts the main series of interactions with the soil. It is important to remember that the root is alive. Its cells are just as active as those of the leaf, but, being in the dark, the root is unable to carry out the energy-fixing process of photosynthesis. Roots are constantly growing, especially the fine rootlets that are effectively foraging for water and minerals in the soil, and these need to be supplied with energy to keep up their activities. This means that there must be a constant supply of sugars from the leaves, passing down the phloem tissues of the stem and right into the root extremities. The absorption of water and dissolved minerals actually takes place through root hairs, which are tubular outgrowths of the surface cells of the roots, most abundant and active just behind the growing tip of the root. One estimate claims that a young (four-month-old) cereal plant has around 14 billion root hairs. Placed end to end, these would stretch for 6,000 miles (10,000 km), the distance from San Francisco to Moscow. This massive production of root hairs shows how much effort the plant expends on the acquisition of water and minerals and how important this process is to the survival of the plant.

The life span of a root hair is only a few days at most. So there is a constant shedding of dead hair cells from the surface of the root. But this effort is not entirely wasted, because the soil around the root is thus supplied with a mass of dead cells in which fungi and bacteria thrive. This benefits the plant because all of these active microbes produce acidic waste products, including carbon dioxide, and their constant digestion of soil materials releases soluble materials that the plant can absorb. There is, in effect, a thin zone of high microbial activity surrounding the root, called the *rhizosphere.* There is a kind of symbiotic association between roots and microbes, the roots supplying energy-rich foods for the microbes in the form of dead cells, and the microbes recycling and releasing the nutrient elements (phosphorus, potassium, calcium, and so on) that are needed by the plant.

Both the roots and most of the microbes need oxygen to respire. In respiration the living cells use oxygen to break down food resources, such as sugars, to produce energy, enabling them to grow and carry out their work. The structure of the soil is very important in controlling the supply of oxygen to the roots and their associated microbes, because air containing oxygen must diffuse through the soil pores from the atmosphere above. The same porous system in the soil permits carbon dioxide, the waste product of respiration, to diffuse out into the atmosphere, where it can be reused by the green plants in their photosynthesis. If there are few pores in the soil, or if they become blocked with excess water, gaseous diffusion is greatly slowed down, and respiration of roots and microbes is made difficult. Some microbes can continue their activities even in the absence of oxygen (anaerobic bacteria), and some plants are more tolerant of anaerobic conditions than others. Rice, for example, is able to grow in waterlogged soils where oxygen is scarce. But most crop plants are killed if their roots become starved of oxygen for long periods.

The "soil atmosphere" is very similar to the atmosphere above the soil surface in its constituents. It consists largely of nitrogen (around 79 percent) and oxygen (about 21 percent), together with small amounts of carbon dioxide and other trace gases. As noted, the carbon dioxide level may rise because of all the respiration that goes on underground. Nitrogen, the main constituent of the soil atmosphere, is a relatively inert gas; it does not react chemically with other compounds at all easily. There are bacteria that live in the soil, however, that are able to trap the nitrogen gas and to combine it with oxygen and hydrogen to make organic compounds called amino acids. These are a vital component of all living things because they are the building blocks of proteins. The microbes that "fix" nitrogen in this way include some free-living bacteria, blue-green bacteria (cyanobacteria), and some symbiotic bacteria that live in the roots of plants (including pea family species, but also such plants as alder, cycads, and others). This process is of immense importance to plants, because nitrogen compounds are vital to their survival and plants are incapable of tapping the atmospheric source on their own. Since all of these "nitrogen-fixers" need to have access to the atmosphere for their supply of nitrogen, the free movement of gases through the soil is necessary for their function. They become inactive if the soil pores become blocked or waterlogged. Indeed, there are some microbes that break down nitrogen compounds back into nitrogen gas if the soils become short of oxygen.

Farmers plow their fields in an attempt to mix air into their soils and to prevent soils compacting and losing their porosity. But there are organisms in the soil that do precisely the same job, namely the earthworms. These invertebrate animals feed on the organic matter in the soil, ingesting soil at one end, digesting some of the materials in the gut, adding mucus and saliva to the mix, and then casting out the waste material, often on the soil surface. Both the tunnels and the broken-up, particulate form of the waste they produce play a very important part in cycling the soil and in maintaining a well-aerated soil.

The same pores that carry the atmosphere into the soil are also the corridors along which water passes on its way through soil. In most temperate areas of the world, water is received as rainfall or melting snow and passes down through the soil on its way to saturated rocks below (aquifers) or to streams and rivers before entering the oceans. In areas of high evaporation, such as the world's arid lands, water may move in the opposite direction, evaporating from the surface and passing upward through the soil. Just as the structure of a soil affects air movements, so it also affects water movements. In a freely drained, sandy soil, water may be able to pass through the soil without any obstruction. This prevents the problems associated with waterlogging, but if the passage of water is too efficient, it can leave the plants without a water supply. Plants are best served by an intermediate set of conditions, where much of the water drains out of the soil under the influence of gravity, leaving open pores for air penetration, but sufficient water is retained in the soil to provide for the needs of the plant. This water is held in the finer spaces within the soil by a property called *capillarity*. Water has a surface tension that causes it to cling to the sides of fine tubes, even rising against the force of gravity. It is this capillary water that forms the main resource of the plant roots, for they can exert a suction force upon these water supplies that can draw them out of the pores and absorb them through the root hairs.

What is clear from these considerations is that the structure (the physical arrangement) of soils is as important as their chemistry in determining how well plants, including

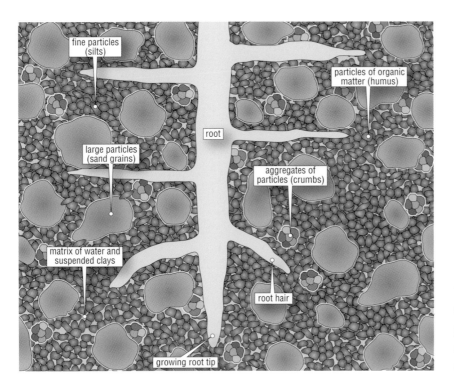

The tip of a plant root, with root hairs, penetrating the soil. The root hairs absorb water and minerals.

arable crops, can grow. One factor that affects the physical conditions of a soil is its texture. This means the proportions of different particle sizes within the soil. The size of particles that make up the soil affects its porosity and therefore its drainage and its air supply. Particle sizes are defined by soil scientists according to the following classification system. Metric units are used in these definitions; one millimeter is approximately equal to 0.04 inches.

The texture of a soil is then described according to the predominance of any of these particle sizes, so a soil may be a clay soil or a sandy clay soil or a silty soil, depending on the major particle. A soil with a relatively even mix of particles is

Particle size classification

More than 2 mm	stones
0.2–2.0 mm	coarse sand
0.02–0.2 mm	fine sand
0.002–0.02 mm	silt
Less than 0.002 mm	clay

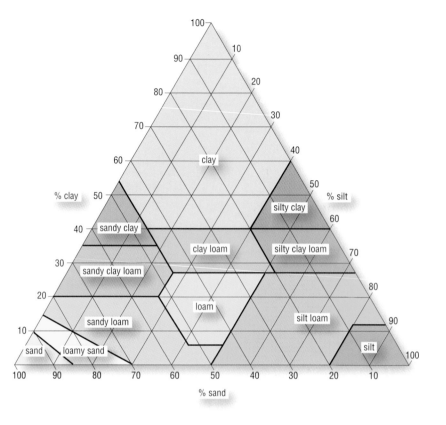

Triangle of texture. This diagram is used by the U.S. Department of Agriculture to classify soils according to the texture (soil particle sizes). The three axes represent the percentage of clay, silt, and sand, respectively.

called a loam. Deviations from the loam condition may be described, for example, as a silty clay loam, or a sandy clay loam, and so on, as shown in the figure. Information about a soil's texture can thus provide a good indication of its properties, particularly its drainage characteristics. The definition of texture types is determined by the proportions of the different particle sizes, and this is best illustrated in a triangular diagram, as shown in the figure.

Large particles in a soil lead to the presence of large pores and give better drainage. If the pores are greater than about 0.05 mm in diameter, then water will drain from them freely under the influence of gravity. If pores are less than 0.0005 mm in diameter, on the other hand, water is held tightly by capillary forces and surface tension and is very difficult to extract. In between these two, water may be retained against the force of gravity but is available to the roots of plants that are able to generate sufficient suction (as a result of the evaporation of water from their leaves) to pull the water from the soil pores and into the root hairs.

Of the various particles within the soil, the clay fraction demands special attention because it behaves in a manner that is of particular significance for plants and their nutrient supplies. Silts and sands are composed mainly of quartz, an inert residue resulting from the weathering of the rock, but clay is much more complex and more reactive in its nature. Clays are crystalline materials that consist of a series of layers of aluminum oxides alternating with silicon oxides to form a kind of multiple-layer sandwich. This unusual structure gives the clay crystal a negative electrical charge over its surface, which results in some remarkable properties. One distinctive feature of clay is that when mixed with water it remains suspended and does not readily sediment to the bottom. (This property provides a convenient technique for the separation of clays from larger particles.) The ability of clays to remain in suspension is partly due to the charges on their surfaces, because the negative charge on each particle repels surrounding particles and holds them at a distance, rather like magnets with like poles facing one another. But it is possible to neutralize the negative charge by adding an excess of material containing atoms, or groups of atoms that are positively charged. Charged atoms, or groups of atoms, are called *ions,* and they can be positively or negatively charged. If we add salt (sodium chloride) to the clay suspension, the positively charged sodium ions will attach themselves to the negative charges on the clay surface and neutralize them, so that the clay *flocculates,* that is aggregates, falls out of suspension, and settles on the bottom. This can be an important process in agricultural soils. If seawater floods an area of cultivated soil, it can lead to the flocculation of the clays in the soil. The result can be a collapse in the structure of the soil, and it may take many years for soils in an area affected by sea flooding to recover.

The negative charges on clay particles have additional significance for soils and the plants they support. Although a massive quantity of positively charged ions can cause the collapse of clay, small quantities actually stick onto the surface of the clay crystals and are loosely held there. We have already seen that many elements are released into the soil by the weathering of the parent rock, and these are supplemented by the breakdown of organic debris in the soil. The positively charged ions can be trapped, or *adsorbed,* by the clay particles, and these include potassium (K+), calcium (Ca++), magnesium (Mg++), and ammonium (NH4+) ions. All of these are required by plants, but can the plant recover them from their location on the clays, or are they too firmly held there? The answer to this question involves the rhizosphere, the zone around the root hairs where bacteria are abundant and active. The high level of microbial activity in the rhizosphere generates acids, including carbonic acid from dissolved carbon dioxide. Acids release hydrogen ions (protons), which are positively charged (the definition of an acid is a compound that releases protons on dissociation), and these positively charged ions are able to dislodge other positively charged ions from the clay particles. So hydrogen replaces potassium, calcium, and other ions from the clays, and they return into solution in the soil water around the root hairs, from which they are taken up by the plant.

The clay component of a soil thus acts as a storehouse for many of the mineral elements needed by plants and offers some protection for these elements, which would otherwise be lost to the soil in solution, passing through with the water draining under the influence of gravity. Despite this activity of the clay, some ions will be lost in this way, a process called *leaching*. If water draining through the soil is particularly acid in nature, then it can even steal ions from the clay surface

Clay particles are extremely small (represented by the hexagons), and their crystalline structure gives them a negative electrical charge (indicated by the minus signs). The negative charge attracts positively charged ions, such as calcium (Ca++), sodium (Na+), hydrogen (H+), potassium (K+), and magnesium (Mg++), and these ions adhere to the clay particles, neutralizing their overall surface charge.

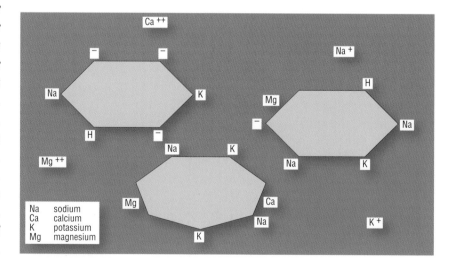

and take them out of the reach of plant roots. This is one of the reasons why the increasing acidity of rainfall in regions of industrial air pollution can be damaging to soils.

Clays are not alone in being able to hold charged ions in the soil. Organic matter also has this property. Organic matter, or *humus,* is the partial breakdown product of living materials, and thus humus is extremely complex in its biochemistry. Like the clays, some portions of the organic matter have a negative surface charge and are likewise able to adsorb positively charged ions on their surfaces. So here is a second store of mineral ions that the plants can tap, again with the assistance of the microbes that surround their roots. Because of this property of humus, gardeners and agriculturalists regard organic matter as a valuable addition to soils and often add compost to soils in order to improve their mineral-holding capacity. Humus is also capable of holding water in the soil, an additional advantage, especially in sandy, well-drained soils. Gardeners and horticulturalists often add peat, a particular type of organic material derived from bogs and recovered by draining the bog and stripping off the peat cover. (Conservationists generally disapprove of this practice, however, because the peat from these unique wetland habitats may have taken many thousands of years to form and cannot be replaced within any reasonable timescale. It is far better to use organic matter from leaf litter or from bark strippings taken from the trunks of trees used in forestry, because these are renewable resources.)

Soil, as can be seen from this brief account, is a very complicated material. It is the site of vibrant activity on the part of animals, plant roots, and microbes, all making a living in this dark, moist world. It is also among the most valuable materials on the surface of the Earth, for it supports the plants that ultimately form the base of all terrestrial food webs. Soil is the basic resource of agriculture; it is here that geology impacts strongly upon global food production.

Soils, climate, and the growth of crops
Although soils are so important in supporting plant growth, it is climate (especially temperature and precipitation) that

ultimately controls the vegetation of a region. It limits what crops can be grown in an area that has been converted to arable agriculture. Climate also has a strong influence on soils, influencing such processes as weathering and leaching, and also operating by its effect on the vegetation cover, which in turn determines the type of organic matter that is fed into the soil from above. Within a given climate, however, soils may vary according to the parent rock material and with such factors as slope and aspect (the direction a slope is facing). Just as different crop species have their specific climatic requirements, so they have their preferences for soil conditions.

How much water is retained in a soil depends not only on the rate of supply from precipitation and from drainage into a site, but also upon the soil texture (proportions of different particle sizes) and the topography (hillcrest, slope, valley floor, and so on). Some crops are sensitive to drought, while others are sensitive to excess water, so either the type of crop grown must be varied according to the soil conditions, or the soil conditions have to be altered to suit the crop. In practice, both processes are used in agriculture. Relatively few crop species are tolerant of high water tables in a soil, so many temperate areas have been subjected to drainage in order to lower the water level and make conditions more suitable for the crop. Generally, the water table should be around three feet (1 m) below the soil surface for healthy crop growth. This can be achieved by a number of means. Ditches dug in the ground to a depth of three feet will carry off surface water and lower the water table. But water may not move into the ditches very rapidly, depending on the permeability of the soil, so waterlogging can persist if the ditches are not close enough together. Underground drains can be used, such as ceramic pipes or perforated plastic pipes that take water from the soil and lead it rapidly away. A less permanent but cheaper method is to use mole drains. These are underground earth tunnels that can be dug with a mole plow that is pulled through the soil without great disturbance to the surface.

With the use of such devices, even low-lying land with clay soils can be reclaimed for crop growth. An alternative in such a wet situation, however, may be the growth of pasture grass and the grazing of animals. But even pasture may need drainage if the productivity of the grasses is to be maximized and if the invasion of wet "weed" species, such as rushes and willows, is to be avoided. An ancient system of managing wet grassland is the construction of water meadows. Alternating ridges and ditches allow water to flood over the riverside meadow in early spring, and this has the effect of warming soils that would otherwise be subject to frost. The outcome of the flooding is that the grasses begin their growth earlier in the season.

At the other end of the spectrum, a soil may be too well drained or have too little supply of moisture to sustain productive crop growth. In this case, the farmer will wish to irrigate the crop rather than drain the soils. The dry lands of the world may come to mind when one thinks of irrigation, but excessive drought is often a problem even in the cooler temperate regions. On a dull day in summer, a New England cornfield may lose as much as 12 tons of water per acre (30 tonnes/ha). This is a lot of water to take out of the soil if there is no replacement going on. Worldwide, the need for irrigation is great. Around 670 million acres (270 million ha) of land are being irrigated, and the supplies of freshwater for this purpose are becoming increasingly scarce. Freshwater may ultimately be the limiting factor for food production on Earth and, therefore, the limiting factor for the expansion of human populations.

Irrigation may be supplied by the channeling of water into the crop, as in the case of the water meadows, by spraying from above, by trickling supplies through pipes that deliver the water directly to the individual plants, or by fitting underground pipes that feed water to the roots. The first two methods (especially the second) are widely used but are also very wasteful, as much of the water supplied evaporates straight back into the atmosphere. The other two methods are more expensive to install but are more efficient to run, so they are increasingly favored where water is expensive, such as in Israel and other arid regions. Water is effectively drip-fed to the plants at the rate they actually require it.

Besides water, the other main requirement of plants from the soil is a supply of nutrient elements, including phosphorus,

Crop rows in an agricultural field. Crop planting ensures that individual plants are well spaced so that they do not compete with one another for light, water, or soil nutrients. (Courtesy of Fogstock)

nitrogen, potassium, calcium, and magnesium. Soils vary in their content of these elements according to the chemistry of the parent rock, the rate of leaching, and the capacity of the soil to retain the elements once they are released by weathering (or microbial decomposition) into solution. This retentive capacity, as discussed earlier in this chapter, is closely related to the clay and humus content of the soil, because these components hold on to ions. Agriculturalists may find it necessary to add organic matter to the soil to improve its nutrient- and water-holding capacity. Traditionally, this has been done by using compost or animal dung in mixed farms where such materials are available.

Natural ecosystems have a recycling system for nutrients that operates through the decomposition of dead plant materials, but agricultural ecosystems are subjected to regular harvesting and this removes elements from the soil. (More will be said of this in chapter 3.) If the rate of element removal exceeds the rate of weathering from the mineral fragments in the soil, it becomes necessary to supplement the nutrient supply by artificial means. In other words, we need to apply fertilizers.

Sometimes there may be too much of certain chemical elements in the soil. This often happens where irrigation is being applied, especially in arid conditions, when evaporation is strong. The water in the soil moves upward because of the evaporative pull at the surface, and salts dissolve in the water on its way up. When the water evaporates at the surface, the salts are left behind and can become concentrated in the surface layers of the soil, precisely where the plant roots are located. There are several salts that can be involved in this process, including common salt (sodium chloride), magnesium chloride, calcium carbonate, and calcium sulfate (gypsum). Gypsum can form a hard concretion on the surface of the soil that is almost impermeable to roots or water, so that even the rain may run off the surface and never soak into the soil. The buildup of salts in a soil is called *salinization*.

Crops vary in the degree to which they can cope with salinity or with raised chemical concentrations in the soil. Some, such as wheat, barley, cotton, sugar beet, and date palms, are quite tolerant, and these crops are favored in dry countries where irrigation is required. There are many different strains and varieties within each of these species, some of which are more tolerant of salinity than others. In the case of barley, for instance, there are some genetic strains that are very tolerant of high salinity, and much effort is expended on selecting and breeding from such varieties to suit the requirements of saline soils, such as those of Iraq and Iran.

Other crop plants, including rice, cabbage, and broccoli, are moderately sensitive to salinity and are not normally grown where salinization is taking place. Yet others, such as strawberry, apricot, avocado, and groundnut, are very sensitive to salinity, so these are crops that are effectively lost if the soils become saline.

Water for the city

Just as crop plants and domestic animals need water for their survival, so do human beings and so does our industry. When cities were first founded, the water supply from the local river was generally assured, but increasing populations in recent times mean that often the city drinks more water than is locally available. So water, like food, has to be imported from outside. Supplying water to our farms can be difficult and expensive, and the same goes for providing water to our cities and factories.

In the United States our water use is the highest in the world, at 1,400 gallons (5,300 L) per person every day. This figure takes into account not just our personal water use, but the water used to support us in agriculture and industry. If the entire world population demanded this quantity, the global water resources could not support the present population of the Earth. The bulk of U.S. water use is for agriculture (41 percent) and for cooling power plants (38 percent). Industry uses 11 percent and public use is 10 percent. Put together these figures show that more than half of the water used in the United States is consumed in the cities.

The eastern part of the United States is fairly well supplied with water and the resources are still generally considered to be adequate, but the central states and the west are short of supplies. New Mexico, Arizona, Utah, Nevada, and California (especially southern California) are the states most severely affected by water shortage. The use of dams for water collection and storage and the long-distance transfer of water are increasing. Such measures create environmental problems in the form of landscape alteration and loss of areas that may be considered of conservation value. On the other hand, dams can also supply energy in the form of hydroelectric power, as well as recreational facilities, such as boating and fishing.

Water conservation is becoming a matter of worldwide importance. Major dam projects will alter the face of the planet in many parts of the world in the near future. India has ambitious plans to construct both large and small dams, collecting in particular the waters that fall over the Himalaya mountain chain and pass through dry lands on their way to the sea. China has plans to construct the world's largest dam and reservoir on the Yangtze, which will create a lake stretching 370 miles (590 km) up the valley. The dam itself will be 600 feet (180 m) in height, and the water supply captured should be adequate to provide for the needs of 150 million people.

Conclusions

The rocks that underlie an area affect the form of the landscape, and the landscape has had a major impact on the development of agriculture and the locations of cities. The nature of the geology of a region affects the location of rivers, which was often of importance for the founding of cities by providing communication links and drinking water. Cities need the raw materials of the rocks for their building materials, and in days of poor transport cities needed a ready supply of these materials in their vicinity. Newly established cities have been less dependent on local rocks, however, because they have made use of concrete as a major building material. Many cities needed a range of geological resources for their industries, including iron, coal, and limestone.

Geology is a major determinant of the kind of soil that prevails in a region, and this is an important aspect of agricultural development. The rock type influences the nature of the particles in the soil and also affects its chemical constitution, especially what elements are available to plants. The clay fraction of a soil is of particular importance because it acts as a reservoir of mineral elements that can be tapped by plant roots. But soils function most effectively if there is a range of particle sizes (a loam soil) because this will ensure the effective drainage of the soil and the penetration of air into the soil. Soils can be improved in their agricultural productivity by the artificial addition of fertilizers or organic matter, and also by draining or irrigation, depending upon the particular requirements at a given site.

CHAPTER 3

FARMS AND CITIES AS ECOSYSTEMS

The idea of the ecosystem is basic to ecology. It is a concept that can be applied at a whole range of different scales; for example, a small pond can be regarded as an ecosystem, as can an area of forest, a single decaying log, or even, at its grandest scale, the whole Earth. Really, the ecologist can draw a line around anything that contains living organisms and call it an ecosystem.

The concept of the ecosystem

What is it that makes the concept of ecosystem special? The most important feature of an ecosystem is that it contains both living and nonliving components, and the study of ecosystems involves discovering how these two components interact with each other. A plant in an ecosystem traps energy from sunlight through the process of photosynthesis. It also takes in the gas carbon dioxide from the atmosphere and uses the energy from sunlight to build the carbon atoms into more complicated and energy-rich sugars. It takes in other elements from the soil, including nitrogen, phosphorus, calcium, and potassium, and uses these in its construction of other compounds, such as proteins and nucleic acids. When the plant dies, its tissues may be used as a source of energy by bacteria and fungi, and the energy is eventually lost into the surroundings as heat (see the sidebar "Measuring energy" on page 60). The elements that were built into the plant tissues will also be released in a nonliving form, but while energy is simply dissipated into the surroundings, these elements will remain in the system and will be available for recycling. Thus the plant interacts with its nonliving environment by exchanging energy and chemical elements with that environment.

Measuring energy

Energy is defined as the ability to do work. There are several units in which energy is expressed, but one that is frequently used in science and in nutrition studies is the *calorie*. A calorie is the amount of energy (in the form of heat) that is needed to raise the temperature of one gram of water by 1°C. This is a very small unit, so energy is more often expressed as kilocalories (kcals). This is the energy needed to raise the temperature of 1,000 grams of water by 1°C (approximately equal to 1.2 pounds or 1.15 pints of water being raised by 1°F). Sometimes energy is recorded in joules. One calorie is equivalent to 4.184 joules.

An animal in an ecosystem also needs energy and chemical elements to grow and reproduce. Animals cannot fix their energy from sunlight and cannot take up carbon dioxide and make it into sugars, so they depend on plants to do this job for them. Herbivorous animals consume the plants that have completed all this work and use their materials and energy directly. They may take in whole molecules from the plant as they digest them in their guts, assimilating amino acids, which can be made into proteins, and carbohydrates, which can be stored as body fats or used to generate energy as they are respired. Respiration releases carbon dioxide back into the atmosphere, where it is available for plant photosynthesis once more. But some material passes through the gut of the animal incompletely digested and absorbed, and this is voided into the ecosystem as feces. There are many small organisms, mainly invertebrates that feed on detritus, together with bacteria and fungi, that are able to make a living out of the energy left in these deposits, or from the dead bodies of the animals that eventually fall to the earth. These are the *detritivores* and *decomposers*, which ensure that no energy-rich materials are wasted. As they break down organic molecules and release the energy, they also set free the inorganic components (the calcium, potassium, phosphorus, and so on), which can circulate through the ecosystem once again. Predatory animals and parasites are only one step further along the food chain. They too obtain their energy indirectly from plants, but it has first passed through the bodies of their prey or host organism. All of these end up supplying the needs of the decomposers.

The two processes that link all the living organisms with the nonliving component of an ecosystem, then, are energy flow and nutrient cycling. It is these two universal processes (which take place within a tussock of grass, a coral reef, a tropical forest, or an aquarium, to name just a few locations) that make the concept of the ecosystem so distinctive and so useful. They provide the ecologist with a means of studying any of these systems in the same basic manner and can supply extremely useful information about the way in which an ecosystem works. If we have a good knowledge of the nutrient cycling patterns and energy flow pathways in an ecosystem, then we can understand the functioning of the ecosystem much more effectively. This knowledge gives us the ability to manipulate the ecosystem, to manage it in a way that suits our particular requirements. In farms and cities, where human beings are so central to the operation of the ecosystem, such control is especially important, but it is also valuable in natural ecosystems, where we may wish to manage for enhanced biodiversity or the conservation of particular species.

Exchanges between ecosystems

Ecosystems in general interact with one another and agricultural and urban ecosystems are no exception. No ecosystem can be considered in total isolation from others because there is sure to be some exchange of energy and materials between any ecosystem and its neighbors. In other words, all ecosystems import and export both energy and chemical elements. In some ecosystems, especially farms and cities, these imports and exports are extremely important to their general function, so it is necessary to consider all the ways that inputs and outputs can take place.

The idea of inputs and outputs to ecosystems can best be understood through an example. Take a well-defined and simple ecosystem such as a pond. This ecosystem (unlike a tussock of grass) has a fairly distinct boundary, namely the edge of the water. Within the ecosystem, a range of energy and nutrient movements is taking place. Waterweeds and green algae are the main primary producers, fixing energy that is devoured by consumers such as water snails and microscopic grazing animals. The grazers are consumed by a range of predatory species, ranging from dragonfly larvae to fish, and these in turn may be eaten by birds, such as coots and grebes. All of these defecate and die in the pond, so their chemical elements are recycled and their energy is dissipated. But this is not the whole story. There is likely to be a stream that enters the pond, and this inflow will bring elements (and possibly even animals) from different ecosystems upstream. There may also be another stream that leaves the pond, taking with it some of the ecosystem's produce. Trees may overhang the pond and in the fall they will drop energy-rich leaves into its waters, providing an additional energy and nutrient resource for a range of detritus feeders and decomposers. If the pond is close to a farm where grazing animals are present, then these may come down to drink and leave behind more nutrients than they consume if they deposit their dung in the waters. The feces will contain energy and chemical elements derived from the pastures where they grazed that have now been added to the nutrient capital of the pond. Similarly, the pond may be visited by a heron that will take fish and return to its nest in a nearby wood, where it will feed its young, having removed both energy and nutrients from the pond ecosystem.

This example demonstrates that movements of energy and materials into and out of ecosystems can be quite significant and that any study of an ecosystem should include a "budget" that takes into account the imports and exports that the ecosystem experiences. Constructing such a budget (which will prove particularly significant in the case of cities and farms) is made simpler if all the different ways in which the inputs and outputs can occur are listed by category. Basically, they fall into three major groups: meteorological, biological, and geological.

Meteorological gains and losses

Movements of the atmosphere and the precipitation of rain and snow can bring new materials into an ecosystem or can erode those materials already present. The rainfall itself, even in clean, pure air, contains many dissolved materials. Measurements of the chemical composition of rain and snowfall have been taken from many different locations, and one of the major factors affecting the quantity of chemicals present is the distance from the ocean. An inland location, such as the Appalachian Mountains in eastern North America, has smaller quantities of chemical elements than the coastal region, such as Long Island. The following figures illustrate the differences in annual deposition in rainfall:

Elements	Appalachians	Long Island
Calcium	2.3 pounds/acre (2.6 kg/ha)	8.7 pounds/acre (9.8 kg/ha)
Potassium	1.2 pounds/acre (1.4 kg/ha)	6.5 pounds/acre (7.3 kg/ha)
Magnesium	0.6 pounds/acre (0.7 kg/ha)	17.0 pounds/acre (19.1 kg/ha)
Sodium	1.3 pounds/acre (1.5 kg/ha)	126.2 pounds/acre (141.5 kg/ha)

The ocean's proximity results in rainwater that is much richer in most elements, especially sodium and magnesium. Plants do not need sodium, but animals use sodium in nerve function. Sodium chloride (salt) from the sea, therefore, is more likely to be harmful than helpful to a farmer growing crops, but it can be useful for pastoral farmers. Magnesium is a vital component of chlorophyll, the pigment that traps solar energy in photosynthesis, so it is an essential element for plants, and the supply from the sea is generally a favorable feature.

But the ocean is not the only source of materials in the atmosphere that can be washed out by rainfall. Dust particles from eroded soils and fertilizers spread over crops can be carried by winds and brought down by raindrops. When raindrops form in the atmosphere, the water vapor condenses on small particles (termed *nuclei*) suspended in the air, and carries these to the ground. As they descend, the droplets also attract and cling to additional particles; they are said to "forage" for dust on their way to the ground. So the atmosphere is much cleaner following rainfall, and the additional chemical materials arrive at the ecosystem where the rain falls. Particles can be carried over large distances in this way. For example, dust from the Sahara in Africa can reach South America and northern Europe when it is carried by strong air currents. The fine sand carried in this way is mainly silica, which is not chemically reactive, but the transport of eroded agricultural soils and fertilizers can have considerable effects on distant ecosystems. Industrial output of reactive gases, such as oxides of sulfur and nitrogen, can acidify the atmosphere and the rainfall and can have a widespread impact on other ecosystems (see "Other cycles in the city," pages 94–98). This is an example of an export from an urban ecosystem.

Biological gains and losses

Many animals depend upon more than one ecosystem for their livelihood. They may spend part of their lives or part of the day in one ecosystem and the remainder in another. The heron described previously may catch fish in a pond, hunt frogs in a wet meadow, and nest in a woodland. In Africa the hippopotamus grazes at night on the banks of rivers and then spends the day in the water, where the waste products resulting from its incomplete digestion of the terrestrial vegetation are deposited in the water. Social birds, such as starlings, will feed together on grassland and lawns and then roost together on buildings or in woodland. So, mobile animals may move materials and energy from one ecosystem to another. Although plants are generally not very mobile, some parts of them may be. Falling leaves in the autumn, pollen released in the spring, and fruits that drift in the wind or are carried by animals can find their way from one ecosystem to another.

Human beings are probably the most effective agent the world has ever known for transporting materials and whole organisms from one ecosystem to another, both intentionally and unintentionally. We plant our crops and then harvest them, frequently transporting the harvest of energy and matter from farm to city. We manufacture fertilizers and pesticides and spread them where they do not occur naturally, and many of these may find their way beyond the arable ecosystem where they were intended to be deposited. In many types of ecosystems, especially in the tropical grasslands, we set fire to the vegetation and thus accelerate the process of nutrient movements as well as producing ash and smoke that carries materials between ecosystems. (We shall look at some of these processes later in this chapter in more detail.) It is evident that humans are a major source of biological gains and losses to ecosystems.

Geological gains and losses

Chapter 2 looked at the way in which the rocks themselves break down to release their component parts, a process called weathering. The importance of the process from a nutrient input point of view also varies with the chemistry of the rock and the abundance of the elements that it contains. It also depends on the speed of weathering, which varies from one rock type to another, depending on the durability of the rocks and their resistance to the destructive physical and chemical forces that are constantly assailing them. The rate of entry of elements to an ecosystem by weathering is difficult to measure, and many ecosystem studies have to be content with crude estimates of this input of materials.

The other major geological input of elements (and sometimes energy-rich materials) is through water flow. If an ecosystem, such as a marsh or a pond, has a stream that enters it, this inflow may prove to be a major source of nutrients. Just how significant a source it is will depend upon the size of the watershed that is drained by the stream. If the catchment is large, then there is a greater chance that elements will be dissolved from a wide area and brought in to the receptive ecosystem. The more water that flows, the more nutrients are likely to be introduced. The nature of the geology and the human land use of the watershed will also be important, as these factors will affect the quality of the water that drains into the ecosystem. If forests are being cleared, soils eroded, or fertilizers being spread, then nutrients may be flushed down the stream and into the new ecosystem.

A stream may also leave an ecosystem, carrying with it any excess elements that have not been taken up by the organisms that reside there. Such outflow represents an export of elements, and this source of loss can be particularly important to farmers, because they wish to minimize losses of nutrients from their arable crops. Losses of fertilizers, for example, are economically wasteful for the farmer and can also lead to excessive imports of nutrients to downstream ecosystems, such as rivers and lakes, that are effectively polluted by the unwanted elements. This type of nutrient transport, creating unwanted fertilization, is called *eutrophication.* A similar problem can face the city ecosystem when it deals with waste disposal.

The ecosystem concept, then, is flexible. It can be applied at a wide range of scales and is readily applied to the artificial ecosystems that we humans have constructed, namely cities and farms. Just like natural ecosystems, cities and farms have internal processes of energy flow and nutrient cycling. They also import and export both materials and energy from their surroundings and often exchange materials and energy with one another. By looking at these processes in detail we can see just how our cities and farms function as ecosystems.

Energy flow in farms

The main objective of agriculture, from an ecosystem point of view, is to channel the energy captured by plants into human consumption. In a natural ecosystem, the energy fixed in photosynthesis (primary production) is usually passed along a wide range of possible paths, often interlinked to produce a food web. It is called a web because of its many links and intersections. For example, a blade of grass may be eaten by a grasshopper that is consumed by a shrike, which may then die and be invaded by flies that are preyed upon by a flycatcher that is eaten by a hawk, and so on. The complexity is almost unlimited; the shrike may eat a lizard that has eaten flies that have bred from a dead hawk, for example. This is why the relationships in natural ecosystems are referred to as food webs rather than food chains. A food chain is a simple, linear sequence, where each step is fairly predictable, and this is very unusual in nature.

Nonetheless, in agriculture, the best way to ensure that the maximum amount of energy that has been produced in an ecosystem reaches human consumption is to simplify the food web to a short, linear food chain. The shortest and the simplest food chain is plant crop → human. If we grow, say, lettuce, and consume it directly, then we are acting as grazers (preferably the sole grazers), and all intermediary steps are eliminated. A short food chain is important economically, because at each stage where energy is passed from one organism to another (as when we consume, digest, and assimilate a plant or animal into our own bodies), there is a very high level of waste. Exactly how inefficient such transfers can be varies with different exchanges and organisms, but as a general rule about 90 percent of the available energy is lost at each transfer. So, when we consume our lettuce, we only succeed in obtaining about 10 percent of the energy that is available to us from that source.

If we use a longer food chain, we consequently reduce the efficiency of our energy harvesting even further. The pastoral food chain, for example, grass → cow → human, involves just one further link, but the energy obtained is only 10 percent of the available cow energy, which is only 10 percent of the grass energy. Hence we succeed in harvesting only 1 percent of the original grass energy. This is one of the reasons why a vegetarian diet has a certain appeal; it is energetically more efficient. A short chain, therefore, is energetically preferable to a long one. We would find it very difficult to support a food industry based on eating wolves or tigers because these are top predators that have many energy exchange links lying beneath them in the chain. (This is, however, precisely what we do in our ocean fisheries. Fish species, such as cod and herring, are top predators in the marine ecosystem, so we are harvesting the seas in a manner that is extremely inefficient in energetic terms, and this could well account for why marine fisheries worldwide are in danger of overexploiting fish stocks.) By keeping our farming food chains short and simple we are making the most efficient possible use of the ecosystem.

One inevitable side effect of simplifying food webs into short linear chains is that we become involved in the elimination of all organisms that normally serve to complicate the pattern of energy dispersal. Obviously, we do not encourage those organisms that would occupy our own position in the food chain. Birds that consume the grain we are growing, locusts that feed upon our crops, and wolves that prey readily

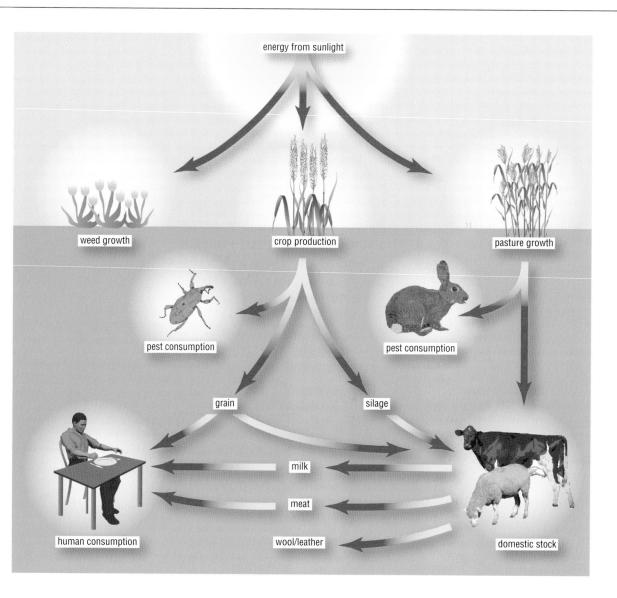

upon our domestic animals (along with all other organisms that could be regarded as our competitors) need to be eliminated if humans are to reap maximum energy from the sources we wish to consume. There are also organisms that compete not with us directly, but with our domesticated plants and animals. What we generally call "weeds" are actually plants that grow where we do not wish them to grow. Often these plant pests are species that compete for light, water, and mineral resources with our domesticated plants, (opposite page) *The course of energy flowing through a farm. Sunlight is absorbed by crop plants and pasture grasses, but also by weeds. Insect pests consume some of the crop productivity, and grazers other than domestic animals take some of the productivity, but some energy finds its way into the human food chain.*

hence reducing their growth and productivity. It is our intention that all available resources should enter our food chain and not be diverted into alternative pathways, so we must rid ourselves of all those organisms that seek the same resources. Similarly, animals that graze upon our crop plants or upon the grasses that feed our sheep and cattle represent side branches in the pattern of energy flow and are to be discouraged. When rabbits consume the energy from rangelands and grasslands that we had intended for human consumption via grazing domestic animals, they set themselves up as our enemies and face our hostile reaction.

When farmers construct short food chains and try to eliminate all side chains, they inevitably create very simple ecosystems. In particular, they deliberately reduce biodiversity to a minimum. As we become "better" farmers (that is, more efficient in the simplification of ecosystems and the diverting of energy into human consumption) so we become more effective in reducing the biodiversity of farmland. Whether this kind of efficiency is actually beneficial in the long term is a question that chapter 4 considers further.

Energy subsidies

Most ecosystems are fueled by the Sun. Almost all of the productivity of the planet is based on the fixation of the energy of sunlight. The exceptions are biologically interesting but are important only locally, for example, the microbes in deep-sea vents that use methane as a source of energy, and the iron bacteria that gain their energy from the oxidation of that element. In the case of agricultural ecosystems, all food chains are based upon the energy of sunlight for their basic functioning. But there is a further matter that we need to consider, namely, the amount of energy we must invest in order to obtain our energy harvest from the ecosystem.

We humans are not alone when it comes to the question of how much energy to invest in order to achieve an energy gain. Consider a honeybee traveling between flowers and gathering nectar and pollen. It is expending a great deal of energy in its activities, but it is also reaping an energy-rich reward in the food it is gathering. If the bee is to survive for any length of time, it must be assured that the amount of energy it gathers equals or exceeds the amount of energy it expends during its foraging. The same applies to humming-birds. They expend very large amounts of energy in foraging and it is only worthwhile if the rewards are plentiful. As a result, most species of hummingbird in North America need to migrate so that they are always assured of abundant sources of nectar-rich flowers. The type of cost-benefit analysis we can apply to bees and hummingbirds applies to all animals, from earthworms to elks, and from marmots to mankind.

Our primitive ancestors were hunters and gatherers. They could survive only if their hunting techniques and the resources they depended on were adequate for the maintenance of their populations. If they were not, then people died and the population fell until a sustainable level was reached. The development of agriculture really stemmed from the idea that the energy invested in gathering and hunting could be reduced if the plants grew together in one place and were thus easily harvested, and the animals people preyed upon could be herded so that the energy spent in hunting could be saved. Growing monocultures of edible plants and managing herds of prey animals led to a massive reduction in the energy normally invested in hunting and gathering and permitted populations to rise. From then on, the greatest concern was increasing the productivity of the domestic plants and animals. In a rather clever twist of domestication, humans learned to use the energy of domestic animals to help in the cultivation of domestic plants. Strong beasts, such as horses and oxen, could be used as an energy resource in preparing land for planting and also in the harvesting process. Horses and dogs could also be used in the hunt, thus increasing the yield per unit of human energy invested. The cost involved was the responsibility to supply the additional energy needs of the helpful animals, which required feeding.

In the last couple of centuries, the quest for yet higher productivity has been greatly assisted by technical and industrial developments. One of these has been the development of methods for producing fertilizers, and the other is the invention of the internal combustion engine.

Artificial fertilizers (see the sidebar) improve the growth and productivity of crops. Along with pesticides, which eliminate weeds, fungi, and harmful insects, chemical fertilizers have significantly increased crop yields.

For its part, machinery has revolutionized agriculture. Like humans and horses, machinery requires energy, but not in the same form as living things. Instead of having to share the products of the land (grain and hay) that were needed for horse power, humans could "feed" machines fossil fuel, a seemingly unlimited resource. Energy, fixed by the process of photosynthesis and laid down many millions of years ago as coal and oil, can be liberated by combustion, and part of the

Artificial fertilizers and energy

In 1909 two German scientists, Fritz Haber and Carl Bosch, invented an industrial means of fixing nitrogen from the air. Until that time, people had to rely on natural biological mechanisms in the soil as the source of nitrogen supply to crops. Certain bacteria have the ability to convert nitrogen gas from the atmosphere into a more usable form of this valuable element. Farmers also conserve nitrogen compounds carefully by recycling the excreta of farm animals into the soil. But the Haber-Bosch process revolutionized agriculture by providing a shortcut so that nitrogen gas could be converted into fertilizer nitrate without the help of microbes. The one drawback is that the process requires very high energy expenditure in the form of fossil fuels. Very high temperatures and pressures are needed to achieve what some bacteria can perform under normal conditions. This means that fertilizer nitrates are expensive in energy. Considering that around 130 million tons of nitrates are produced each year by this method and that about 40 percent of the world's population is now dependent on this process, it is clear that this is one of the major supports for our high human population level. But it is also a major consumer of energy.

energy released can be channeled into doing work. Plowing the fields, spraying pesticides and herbicides, applying fertilizers, constructing irrigation channels, and harvesting the crops were all made much simpler by the use of machinery, involving the consumption of fossil-fuel energy. Although human energy input, in the form of muscle activity, is reduced by these means, energy of another type is still being expended. Fertilizers and pesticides, which are mainly derived from industrial processes, likewise demand further energy investment. These expenditures are known as a fossil fuel "energy subsidy" in agriculture.

The energy of fossil fuels is used to do work on the farm, making use of agricultural machinery. But modern farming also needs fertilizers to improve the growth and productivity of crops and pesticides to eliminate weeds, fungi, and harmful insects. The fertilizers and pesticides that are now spread on our fields are mainly derived from industrial processes, and these demand further energy investment.

Using the ecosystem approach in studying agriculture, the fossil-fuel energy subsidies must be included in the overall budget for the system. As a very simple illustration, we could take a study of a lawn in California that is managed for recreation. Each year the grasses on the lawn have a primary productivity of 3,762 kilocalories per square yard (4,500 kcal/m^2). Leaves also blow onto the lawn from surrounding trees, and these are raked off by the owner. They comprise an energy import of a further 2,090 kilocalories per square yard (2,500 kcal/m^2). Mowing the lawn actually removes a proportion of the primary productivity, amounting to about 418 kilocalories per square yard (500 kcal/m^2). So the total amount of energy removed from the ecosystem by human activity (raked leaves plus mowings) is 2,508 kilocalories per square yard (3,000 kcal/m^2) per year. Much of the energy required to gather this produce, however, is supplied by a gasoline-driven mowing machine, and the fossil-fuel energy consumed in the process is 1,672 kilocalories per square yard (2,000 kcal/m^2) each year. Obviously, in this simple example, the leaves and grass mowings produced by the management of the lawn are of no commercial use or value. But a comparison of the energy extracted from the ecosystem in relation to the amount of energy expended in gathering it shows that 2,508 kilocalories of produce have cost 1,672 kilocalories of energy investment. In other words, we get 1.5 units of energy out of the system for every one unit invested. From an energy balance point of view, therefore, this is a satisfactory system in which we get out more than we put in. If we think of it as an energy-harvesting system, then we are gaining more than we spend.

We can apply the same kind of analysis to an agricultural crop to establish whether the energy subsidy from fossil fuel is being adequately repaid in the product. In order to produce 10 tons of potatoes, for example, we need to expend about 5,000 kilocalories in the form of fertilizer production, spraying, irrigating, harvesting, and transporting. Of that 10 tons, about 10 percent will be needed for replanting as the seed potatoes for next year's crop. Also, around 10 percent is likely to have been spoiled by pests or in the mechanical harvesting process. By the time that further energy has been expended on transport from farm to retail outlet, and more wastage has resulted from washing, packaging, and peeling, the total energy content of the product will be about 6,200 kilocalories. This means that for every unit of energy we invest in the crop in the form of fossil fuel subsidy, we obtain 1.15 units of energy in the form of food. In other words, in energy terms we just about break even. Looking at it in another way, the potato is really a machine that we use for converting fossil-fuel energy into food.

In fact, the potato is one of our more efficient food sources from the energy subsidy point of view. Many other crops require more attention in the form of irrigation, pesticide spraying, fertilizing, and so on. Also, the potato puts quite a lot of its overall energy into the buried stem tuber that we eat; many crops provide only a small proportion of their total productivity in a form that is suitable for human consumption. Animal produce of all kinds demands more energy subsidy in proportional terms because of the energy inefficiency involved in taking energy from a point further along the food chain. The following is a series of energy output-to-input quotients for different types of food.

Coffee: 0.006
Tomatoes: 0.02

Whitefish:	0.03
Fruit:	0.05
Chicken:	0.14
Eggs:	0.16
Lamb:	0.17
Milk:	0.3
Potatoes:	1.15
Wheat:	2.2
Maize (grain):	2.8
Maize (animal feed):	8.9

In the case of corn (maize), we have a very productive and efficient crop, but if we only use the fruit (the grain or corn on the cob) then much of the crop is wasted. If the vegetative parts of the plant are also used, in feeding cattle for example, then the efficiency per unit of fossil fuel invested is clearly greatly increased. As fossil fuels decline and become more expensive through the world, we must move toward less energy-expensive forms of agriculture and methods that will allow us to harvest as much as possible of the produce.

The past century saw the great expansion of mechanized agriculture and the increasing use of fossil-fuel subsidies. Over the same period, as a consequence of this energy subsidy, the actual efficiency of energy extraction has generally decreased. In the United States, for example the energy output-to-input quotients for the entire agricultural system have declined steadily as agriculture has become more and more machine dependent.

United States in 1900:	1.0
United States in 1940:	0.2
United States currently:	0.1

The output-to-input quotients of less mechanized systems of agricultural production present a sharp contrast.

Nigeria (sorghum cultivation using oxen):	0.9
India (wheat using oxen):	1.0
Philippines (rice using buffalo):	3.3
Mexico (maize using oxen):	3.4
African hunter/gatherer cultures:	5 to 10
Sudan (sorghum using human labor):	14.1

Polynesia (farming and gathering):   20.0
Congo (cassava using human labor):   37.5

What is evident from these figures is that crop production using human labor results in an elevation of the energy output for each unit expended. Once animals are used as working assistants, the ratio of output to input falls because of the need to supply the animals with their energy requirements. But this does not mean that the system is less efficient. The total amount of productivity per unit area of land is also an important consideration, perhaps even more important than energy balance, and this is increased by employing animal labor. Similarly, our current levels of food production have been increased as a result of fossil-fuel energy subsidies, so the energy output-to-input quotients are not the sole, or even the most effective, measure of agricultural efficiency. Productivity and economic return are much more important in the view of the farmer. Only when the cost of energy subsidy results in the output being uneconomical will the farmer have to turn to new methods or new sources of energy. The importance of finance and economics in farming means that we cannot look at agriculture simply in ecosystem terms if we wish to understand how it should best be managed.

Harvesting energy

The main objective of farming is to harvest energy from the agricultural ecosystem. This energy is usually in the form of food for human consumption, such as grain, root crops, meat, and milk, but other products may also be produced, such as animal skins for leather and wood for construction or for burning. Whatever the crop, energy is being taken from the ecosystem because all of these products contain energy. We need to ask, then, whether our extractions might take too much energy out of the system and cause it to run down. The answer must take into account two important facts: First, that there is a constant supply of new energy in the form of primary production, fixed from sunlight; and, second, that there is a store, or reservoir, of energy in the ecosystem, the biomass (energy stored within the living organisms) and the soil organic matter. Energy is being lost because all of the

Harvesting grain. The energy that cultivated plants on farms store in their seeds is harvested for human use, often in the city. But energy, in the form of fuel for machinery, has to be expended during the harvest. (Courtesy of Fogstock)

living organisms are respiring and using it up, and also because we are taking some of it away in our harvest. We can think of the agricultural ecosystem as being like a pail with a faucet dripping in water at the top. As the pail fills with water, we can empty it all at once, which is equivalent to taking a single harvest at a certain point in the year. But if we want to take regular crops throughout the year (as when we graze animals on a pasture), our usage is like having a leak in the bottom of the bucket. If the leak is faster than the supply of water from the faucet, then the level of water in the bucket will fall until eventually it is empty. But if we control the leak so that the rate at which water is lost is equaled by the new supply from above, then the level of water will remain the same and we have a stable equilibrium system.

Ideally one should aim to match the rate of consumption with the rate of production in the ecosystem (equivalent to matching the speed of the leak to the speed of the dripping faucet). If we take energy out faster than it is coming in, the reservoir, in this case the biomass of the grass in the pasture, will gradually be diminished. This is known as overgrazing, and it will eventually result in the total devastation of the grass, with just bare soil remaining. Overgrazing is a particular problem where the original biomass and productivity of the rangeland is low, as in the dry lands around deserts. If, on the other hand, the density of grazing animals is too low, the situation is akin to having a slow leak in the pail, allowing the level of water to rise. In other words, the grass biomass would increase because the new input of production is not being consumed. From the farmer's point of view, this is a waste of a resource, because a bigger crop could be harvested (in the form of meat or milk) without any damage to the ecosystem.

In either instance, the simple way to control the energy consumption is to modify the density of animals feeding in the pasture. The more sheep or cattle there are per acre, the more energy is consumed. So the farmer is able to manipulate the energy flow through an agricultural ecosystem by adjusting stock density and can make sure that the harvest is maximized without causing the ecosystem to lose its ability to function. This is what is meant by a sustainable harvest, and this is the aim of all sensible farmers.

Nutrient cycling in farmland

While energy flows through an ecosystem, the elements that compose the material parts of the ecosystem mainly circulate within it. In addition, as we have seen, all ecosystems have inputs and outputs of elements as they move between ecosystems. In the case of agricultural ecosystems, these inputs and outputs are particularly important because they are largely under the control of the farmer, who must ensure that the whole budget for the ecosystem balances. As in the case of energy budgets, the "dripping faucet and the leaking pail" model applies, and an imbalance can lead to the whole system becoming unstable and possibly even collapsing.

Stability is an important concept in ecology, and particularly so in agriculture. It is not easy to measure stability or to define it, but one aspect of stability is that the stable object is not easily moved. A stable ecosystem is one that is not easily damaged or changed in any way. It has the property of inertia. Natural ecosystems can illustrate this property, as in the case of the deciduous forests of the northeastern United States. These forests are relatively resistant to all the pressures that are placed upon them and it takes a lot of effort to change them into different kinds of ecosystems (such as grasslands). The pattern of nutrient cycling plays an important part in establishing this stability, mainly because there is a very large reservoir of nutrients in the plant biomass and in the soil. Take the element calcium as an example. Every acre (0.4 ha) of forest contains 176 pounds (80 kg) of calcium in the trees and a further 320 pounds (145 kg) of calcium that is available to plants in the soil. The loss of calcium from the same area in the drainage water is only about nine pounds (4 kg), and this is replaced by the weathering of rocks and a small input in the rainfall. If we express this annual through-flow of calcium as a percentage of the total resident calcium, then it is less than 2 percent. So it is only a very small proportion of the total calcium reservoir that is on the move in and out of the ecosystem each year. This is a measure of the stability of the system.

It works rather like a bank. If a bank has very large assets of money, then you feel more confident about placing your (relatively small) amount of capital in its care. While the bank has large assets in comparison to the flow in and out, you can be confident that it is stable and your money is safe. Just so with an ecosystem; one with high capital relative to the through-flow is more stable.

In the case of agricultural ecosystems, the opposite is often the case. The biomass of an annual crop, such as wheat, changes every year. The soil remains present, but because of these large withdrawals there is a danger that even the nutrient capital of the soil may become reduced and unstable. In a pastoral ecosystem, the quantity of nutrients being withdrawn is smaller, and the nutrient reservoirs of grass and soil remain relatively intact, so this is likely to be a more stable system.

As in the case of energy, however, the farmer needs to ensure that the stability of an agricultural ecosystem is protected as far as possible by matching the inputs to the outputs, or by ensuring that the removal of any element in the harvest does not exceed the supply from other sources. As explained previously, nutrients enter ecosystems by meteorological, biological, and geological routes. When we take a harvest from the ecosystem, we remove a range of elements, and this may exceed the rate of supply. As an example, consider nitrogen, an important element for all organisms. Nitrogen is vital for life because it is an essential component of proteins and of nucleic acids. Rocks are not a good source of the element, so weathering is not an important input. Although nitrogen is abundant in the atmosphere, it is not immediately available to plants in its gaseous form, but there are some bacteria that are able to convert ("fix") nitrogen gas into a usable form, and most of the nitrate (the usable form of the element) in the soil is derived from bacteria or from the breakdown of organic matter. When we grow a crop, such as barley, and harvest it at the end of the growing season, we remove a significant amount of nitrogen from the soil. From each square yard we may harvest around 0.08 ounces (2.5 g) of nitrogen. At the same time, water moving through the soil and the activity of denitrifying bacteria (which convert nitrates back into nitrogen gas) account for the loss of a further 0.04 ounces (1.4 g). So, at the end of the season, the soil has been depleted of its nitrate content. The simple answer to the problem, and the one most frequently adopted, is to add fertilizer artificially, either as chemicals that have been manufactured by industrial methods (such as the Haber-Bosch process; see "Artificial fertilizers and energy" page 71) or as organic matter (animal dung, sewage sludge, and so on). Whichever is used, the nitrogen ends up as nitrate in the soil. The most important consequence is that the yield is increased. If we add, say, 0.32 ounces (10 g) of nitrogen in this form to each square yard, then the most important consequence is that the yield of the crop is greatly increased, up to 0.32 ounces (10 g) instead of the original 0.08 ounces (2.5 g) for the nitrogen output in the harvest. This is because nitrate is in such short supply in the soil that the crop plant efficiently taps in on the new supply. The other losses, by solution in drainage water and by bacterial action, remain the same, and the overall outcome is that the soil loses less of its own nitrogen reservoir.

Adding fertilizers, therefore, can certainly increase crop yield, but it does not necessarily fully prevent the problem of soil impoverishment. An alternative approach is to give the soil a rest periodically and grow a different crop. Perhaps the arable field could be turned over to grass for a few years, allowing natural bacterial fixation of nitrogen to take place and the organic matter in the soil to accumulate. Or, even better, a crop that fixes its own nitrogen could be grown. Members of the pea family have developed a close relationship with a group of bacteria that can fix atmospheric nitrogen. These microbes live in the roots of the plant, in small lumps, or nodules, upon them. Safe inside these nodules, the bacteria are also supplied with their food in the form of sugars that the plant has manufactured by photosynthesis, and in return they pass on some of the nitrogen that they fix into a plant-usable form. Several pea-family plants can be used to replenish the soil reserves of nitrogen, including peas, beans, clover, and alfalfa (lucerne). In one season a crop of alfalfa can inject more than one ounce of nitrogen into each square yard (38 g/m^2). Much of this can be harvested at the end of the season and used as a source of fodder, but even if 0.75 ounces (25 g) are removed in this way, it still leaves an extra 0.3 ounces (11 g) to accumulate in the soil and replenish its reserves. If instead the crop is not harvested, but plowed back into the soil, then even larger stocks of nitrogen can be built up. (This may be moderated, however, by a faster rate of loss of nitrate in the water flow, because large quantities of nitrate are not easily stored in soils.) The idea of crop rotation was developed first in England in the 18th century and caused a revolution in the agriculture of that time.

Slow-growing perennial crops, such as trees used for timber or fuel production, present a slightly different problem from those of annual crops. The harvest may be taken only once every 20 years or so. We then need to check whether the nutrients removed in the final harvest are replaced over this relatively long period by natural inputs (from rainfall, weathering, and so on) or whether further fertilizer addition is required. In Belize in Central America, for example, crops of pine are harvested periodically from the light, sandy, nutrient-poor soils. Weathering produces very little nutrient replacement in this situation, so the major natural source of elements to replace the harvested elements is rainfall. Analysis of the chemistry of the rainfall shows that, over the life span of the pine up until harvesting, all the required potassium and almost half the calcium, magnesium, and phosphorus needed by the growing trees can be replaced by the rainfall alone. In a situation where the industry needs to economize on fertilizer expenses, this is an important fact to know. It means that if the unwanted branches and leaves are stripped from the trunk timber and left behind to decay after the harvest, then the additional inputs from rainfall will be adequate for the growth of the new crop, and no additional fertilizer is required. Efficient, sustainable harvesting, therefore, demands a detailed knowledge of nutrient cycling.

Where animals or their produce (eggs, milk, wool) are being harvested from a pastoral ecosystem, it is still necessary to check the balance of nutrient inputs and outputs. Harvesting animals, on the whole, involves the removal of much less biomass than in the case of plant harvest, such as cereals or timber. One might expect, therefore, that the harvest is a less serious drain on the nutrient resources of the ecosystem. Where studies have been conducted, this has indeed proved to be the case. One such study was carried out in a mountainous region of northern England, where sheep were regularly harvested (for both meat and wool production) from an area of very poor soils and high rainfall. It showed that the quantity of phosphorus being lost from the ecosystem by the harvesting of sheep and wool each year amounted to less than 2 percent of the amount of phosphorus arriving in annual rainfall. In other words, the rainfall alone (quite apart from other sources, such as rock weathering) provides 50 times the phosphorus required for the maintenance of the harvest. Similar figures were found for other nutrient elements. The removal of animal products from this system, therefore, has a negligible impact on the nutrient cycles and is indefinitely sustainable without additional fertilizer inputs. If fertilizers are added to the grassland, however, they are likely to increase the land's productivity, which would allow the density of animals, and hence the harvest, to be increased.

Energy in the city

Examined from the point of view of energy flow, cities are very unusual ecosystems. They consume far more energy than they produce. In some respects a city is like a stream, for

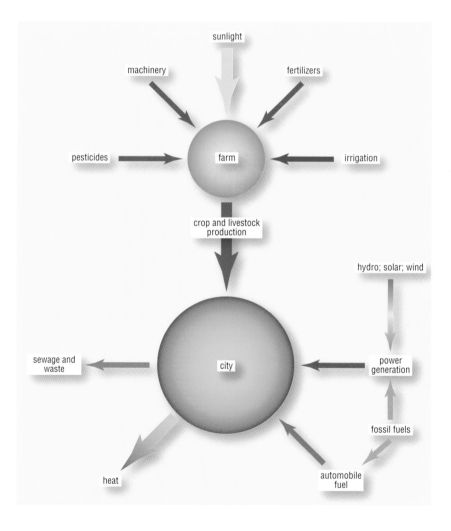

The flow of energy through farms and cities. The total energy input to farms and cities includes not only sunlight but also energy derived from fossil fuels and other sources of power. Much of the food energy produced in the farm is passed on to the city, where it eventually dissipates as heat.

there is very little energy production by photosynthesis in a stream; most of the energy arrives from other ecosystems in the form of leaves and other plant detritus, and this is the principal energy supply for all the animals that live in the stream. Similarly, in the city, there may be some photosynthesis from trees, grasses, and garden plants, but these only support local communities of animals. The main biomass of the city is human, and people obtain their energy from other ecosystems. The food energy needs of the city dweller are supplied by the farms, and we have to look to fossil fuel or additional sources of energy for the maintenance of our other energy-demanding activities, such as travel, heating, lighting, air-conditioning, and so on.

Nonfood energy

Cities consume large quantities of energy in order to keep functioning. Offices, houses, and highways need to be lit at night. Dwellings and workplaces need to be heated when the outside conditions are cold and cooled when conditions are hot. Cities depend upon the movement of people within them, bringing workers from the residential zones and shoppers to the retail outlets. Raw materials, including food, industrial materials, and sales goods, must be moved into cities, and industrial products need to be exported. Rapid communication systems need to be maintained through telephone, radio, and television. All of these things that we take for granted require energy for their function, and that energy has to be imported into the city because the city cannot produce energy for itself. Cities vary in just how much energy they consume, but an average American city of 1 million inhabitants consumes about 9,500 tons (8.6 million kg) of fuel (oil and coal) each day.

There are many possible sources that the city can draw upon, some of them *renewable,* in the sense that more energy is being formed to replace that which we use. Some sources of energy are *nonrenewable,* meaning that once we have used them they cannot be replaced. Over the centuries our cities have shifted between different energy resources. Before about 1875 the major source of energy in the United States for the

The production of energy in the city. A smokestack releases the waste products of fuel combustion as fossil materials are burned to release their energy for human use. (Courtesy of Fogstock)

general demands of human living was wood. This is a renewable energy resource because it is derived from sunlight through the photosynthesis of trees. But it is also a rather bulky form of energy that does not lend itself to easy transport and storage. By 1875 in the United States it was rapidly being replaced by coal, but in some parts of the world wood is still a major energy resource. In the developing world many cities are still highly dependent on wood fuel as an energy resource, especially for space heating and cooking. The poorer residential zones of developing-world cities, such as Kampala in Uganda or Lucknow in India, are distinctive for their smell of wood smoke in the evenings as fires are used for the cooking of meals.

The shift to the use of coal in the United States peaked in the early part of the 19th century. Coal could be mined and transported relatively easily, and it formed the basis for steam locomotive travel and the generation of electricity for a range of other energy-expensive activities. It was coal that had literally fueled the industrial revolution in 18th-century Europe, and this fossil fuel remained the staple energy resource of the developed world until around 75 years ago. Like wood, coal is an energy resource that is based upon the energy of sunlight that has been trapped by photosynthesis, but in the case of coal that energy has lain buried and dormant for millions of years. It consists of plant remains from ancient tropical swamps that have been fossilized and compacted beneath layers of rocks, retaining their energy content until they were eventually brought to the surface and combusted (burned) by humans. Unlike wood, therefore, coal cannot be replaced once it has been used up; it is a nonrenewable energy resource.

As the resources of coal became scarcer, they became more expensive to extract from the ground, so people sought a cheaper alternative. Oil and gas are alternative fossil energy resources that have proved extremely valuable to humans. By 1950 the United States was using more energy in this form than coal. Oil and natural gas were also formed by photosynthetic organisms many millions of years ago. Oil can be pumped out of the ground rather than mined, and this has made it attractive as a relatively easily recovered and easily transported source of energy. Natural gas is less easy to handle, and in the Middle East, where both oil and gas are relatively plentiful, the costs of extracting and transporting gas are greater than the market value of the commodity. Consequently, the gas that accompanies oil in the underground reserves is simply burned off as it reaches ground level. This is a waste of energy and also a source of atmospheric carbon dioxide, but economics currently dictate that this should be the way to deal with it. In general, oil and natural gas contain less of the pollutant sulfur than coal, so they are cleaner to use and less likely to pollute the atmosphere. But they do still produce carbon dioxide as a waste product of combustion, and this greenhouse gas becomes added to the atmosphere. (For more on this topic, see "Other cycles in the city," pages 94–98.) Also like coal, oil and gas are nonrenewable resources; once we have used up the reserves around the world, they cannot be reconstructed.

Cities are not alone in importing fuels for energy. As we have seen, farmlands import fossil fuels and use them as an energy supplement in agriculture. But farmlands still depend mainly on solar energy to fuel their crops, while in the cities local photosynthesis is effectively irrelevant and the important energy input comes either as fossil fuels or as electricity mainly generated from fossil fuels. Cities will always be dependent on imported energy, so as the supplies of nonrenewable energy decline (likely over the next 50 years), other energy sources must be discovered and exploited if the cities are to avoid extinction.

One alternative source of energy is nuclear energy. Nuclear energy has been used in several parts of the world, and this source has the advantage that it does not produce carbon dioxide, so it does not add to the greenhouse warming of the planet. But it does produce other waste products that are more dangerous and more difficult to dispose of. There is also a very real possibility of accidental meltdown of the nuclear reactor. In this situation, the nuclear reaction that generates the energy goes out of control, leading to an excessive buildup of heat and the danger of explosion. Although the likelihood of this occurrence is very low and depends on a coincidence of errors, it has been known to happen, as at Three Mile Island in the United States in 1979 and at Chernobyl in what was then the Soviet Union, in 1986. Statisticians have calculated that there is a 70 percent probability of a further serious accident within about five years. The release of radioactive materials from such an accident is very harmful, so the future of nuclear energy needs to be carefully considered.

Several other possible sources of renewable energy are available, but all will present technical problems of development and harnessing if they are to replace our dependence on fossil fuels. Solar energy is an easily available source, but the efficiency of current methods of trapping it is still low. Biomass use involves growing plants as a source of renewable energy. This source has long been used in the form of firewood, but a more convenient way of using biomass is to ferment it to produce alcohol that can be used as a substitute for gasoline. A problem with this source is that it would take large areas of agricultural land to produce sufficient biomass to support the current human population. Urban organic waste could be incinerated to recover energy. The wind and the tides release much energy that could be harnessed by humans; already the flow of water from land to sea has proved a rich source of hydroelectric power. Then there is the possibility of using the heat from the Earth's center, geothermal energy. Unlike fossil fuels, all of these are energy resources that will be available until the solar system itself fades away, and the development of strategies for tapping them is an increasingly urgent need. As fossil fuels become scarcer and more expensive, humanity will be driven by economic pressures to research more extensively into these alternatives.

Food energy

Cities in general do not produce their own food requirements; they need to import food from the rural countryside. Some city dwellers may grow some home produce for their own consumption, but in the cities of the developed world, this is a negligible source of food energy for the city as a whole. One could, therefore, regard the city as a parasite on the countryside, but this would not be entirely fair. Although the city is dependent on the countryside for food, it is within the city that factories build tractors and other machinery needed by the farmer. The city contains the chemical plants where fertilizers and pesticides are made. The city is the financial center where banks make loans to farmers for the development of new agricultural schemes. It is also the city that provides country dwellers with retail outlets and with cultural and educational resources that they need. Towns and cities may well have evolved simply because there was a surplus of food production, allowing some members of society to become specialized in their activities and providing services to the agricultural producers. So the city is not really a parasite, it is more like a partner in a well-balanced symbiosis, each partner gaining from the relationship. There will, of course, be occasions of disagreement, as when cities demand more land for development or when farmers need more

The food energy of the city. Vegetables produced in farms are transported into the city, where urban populations consume them. Cities are thus dependent on farms for their supply of food energy. (Courtesy of Nikki Ward)

water for irrigation, but the two human-dominated ecosystems usually live in mutual dependence and harmony.

Just as the energy for industry and residential dwellings is imported from outside the city ecosystem, so is the energy required for food. In a typical American city of 1 million inhabitants, the daily import of food amounts to about 2,000 tons (1.8 million kg). In some cities the food may be carried in fresh directly from the surrounding farmland. Vegetables may be brought to central markets from which they are distributed to smaller local outlets. Animals may be herded directly into the town for slaughter and distribution to meat suppliers. In modern cities, where we are accustomed to obtaining our food prepackaged from supermarkets, the urban dweller is separated even further from the labor of food production and processing, distancing the city dweller from the agriculturalist. Food is then brought into the city in a hygienically wrapped form that is quite unrecognizable from the food's original state and is transported in trucks from processing plants that form a link between farm and city.

Food is not the only resource required by the city dwellers. They also need water. Our typical American city with 1 million inhabitants consumes around 150 million gallons (568 million L) of water each day. Like food and energy, water needs to be imported, but if there is a river flowing through the city this can provide an important source. Usually it is necessary to build reservoirs for water storage even when a river is present. Reservoirs are usually situated upstream of the city. Their elevation is an important consideration, because water should flow down under the influence of gravity into the locations where consumers want to use it, saving the energy of pumping. So the altitude of reservoir construction can limit the upward growth of a city; a city cannot grow higher than its water supply unless energy is expended on pumping the water to where it is needed. Another reason why reservoirs are situated upstream is because rivers passing through cities often become polluted by industrial waste and sewage. It may be necessary to draw upon flowing water resources in spite of this pollution, but stringent measures must be taken to ensure that water discharged into rivers has been cleansed and that water subsequently taken from the river is treated to remove chemical and microbial pollutants. It has been estimated that by the time the water of the Thames River in England flows beneath London Bridge in the city, it has passed through eight people.

Water, then, is a precious resource for the city and many urban settlements need to look to distant sources to satisfy their water needs. By 1900 the city of New York had to take water from the Catskill Mountains, 100 miles away. This is a common situation for many modern cities, and some cities that occupy dry regions need to look even farther for their water. Los Angeles, California, for example, was drawing upon the Columbia River, 150 miles away, by 1910, and by 1913 an aqueduct had been constructed to transport the water. So cities may need to build their own rivers to supplement local water supplies. This was a very expensive venture, however, and it was financed by the cooperation of many settlements in the Los Angeles area. As a result, many of these towns became more closely associated and joined into the complicated fusion of towns, which gives Los Angeles its characteristic sprawling form. The construction of an extensive aqueduct was certainly not a new idea. Two thousand years ago the Romans, who occupied regions with a similar climate to that of Los Angeles, were constructing aqueducts to bring water into several of their Mediterranean cities. Applying the same water-gathering techniques to the resources of the Sierra Nevada in northern California, Los Angeles has succeeded in depleting the water supplies of many of the regions on the dry eastern side of the mountains, contributing to desertification in that area.

Where rivers pass through different countries, the competition for water can lead to serious political and ecological problems. The extraction of water from the Jordan River by Israel has led to a fall in the water level and in the geographical extent of the Dead Sea at the river's southern end. In eastern Africa the Nile River passes from its two sources in Uganda and Ethiopia, through the Sudan to Egypt. Many international arguments have resulted because the states upstream of Egypt extract water. Even within Egypt, the construction of the Aswân Dam in the south of the country led to problems in Lower Egypt, where the regular Nile floods were interrupted and agriculture had to adapt to new conditions. In the lands to the east of the Mediterranean, water is scarce and two of the largest rivers, the Euphrates and the Tigris, arise in Turkey and then flow south into Syria and Iraq. It is clearly in the interests of Turkey to store the water and then sell it to the downstream countries or to richer countries such as Saudi Arabia. Water, therefore, is a resource that every city needs and that could prove increasingly difficult to obtain in sufficient quantities to supply the extravagant needs of modern city dwellers. Perhaps freshwater supplies will one day limit how many people can live on the surface of the Earth.

Nutrient cycling in cities

In natural ecosystems many elements are cycled between the living and the nonliving components of the system. A phosphorus atom taken up by a plant, for example, may be passed on to a herbivore, then to a carnivore, and then be excreted or liberated when the animal dies and decays. It is then available in the soil for reuse by plants once more. In the city the pattern of element movement is different. As already discussed, food is all imported, so the main consumer animals, the human beings, obtain their elements from outside the

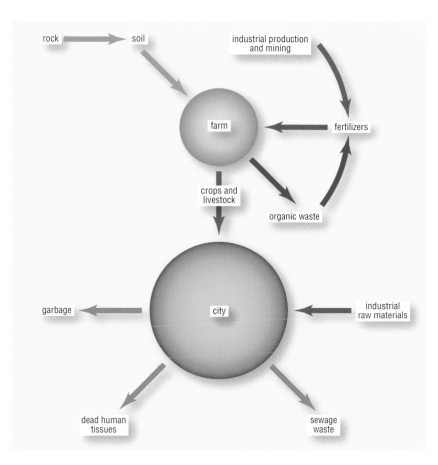

Nutrient movements from farms to cities. The nutrients we need may originate in rocks and soils or may be derived from the atmosphere by industrial processes. Elements supplied to farm crops as fertilizers eventually find their way to human consumption and are returned to the environment in human sewage and waste.

city. Some of the food is wasted, which basically means that it supplies the needs of other animals that we think of as pests. Much passes through our bodies and is released in our sewage output. Urine contains much of the nitrogen that we take in and that we do not really need. Nitrogen is an important component of proteins, and most of us take in much more protein than we actually require to maintain our bodies. The proteins are broken down and used as an energy source, liberating carbon dioxide, but the nitrogen is removed from the bloodstream by the kidneys and converted into a nitrogen-rich compound called urea that is excreted in urine. Fecal material consists largely of undigested or unused food material, together with the populations of bacteria that we harbor in our intestines. These two components of sewage take many elements from the living to the nonliving part of the ecosystem.

The use of sewage as a source of nutrients for agricultural systems is practiced in some countries, such as China. This makes good ecological sense from the point of view of recycling materials that would otherwise create problems in disposal. The main objection to the use of raw sewage as a fertilizer is that it could contain parasites or pathogenic (disease-causing) bacteria and thus present a health hazard to agricultural workers. Some parasites, such as tapeworm and roundworm, rely on poor hygiene for their movement between hosts (humans and pigs in the case of tapeworms), so the use of raw human sewage as an agricultural resource is not widespread in developed countries. When treated to remove harmful organisms, however, it can be used in this way. Alternatively, it is possible to use these materials as an energy source, and several villages in India have biogas facilities that consume sewage and produce methane gas that can be burned as an energy source.

Most sewage is treated within the city, either being transported directly to treatment plants by pipes, or, in the case of some suburban dwellings, being collected in septic tanks and distributed within the soil through perforated pipes. The materials released into the soil in this way are decomposed by soil bacteria and are released for recycling in plants, or are washed through the soil and into streams or other water bodies. It is important, obviously, that the location of septic tank treatment systems should be distant from wells or other sources of drinking water. In the case of major sewage treatment systems, the raw sewage passes through a series of processes. The first of these is sedimentation in which solid matter settles out in tanks. This matter is then treated with bacteria operating in an aerated environment that digest the solid waste. Harmful bacteria are killed in this process and the eventual product can be incinerated, dumped as landfill, or even used as agricultural fertilizer. The wastewater in this process may still contain organic molecules and fine particulate matter. It will also be rich in materials such as nitrates and phosphates that are important nutrients for plants, so the release of this water into rivers or oceans can stimulate the growth of algae or other aquatic plants in a process known as eutrophication. There may also be a residue of toxic materials that are not removed by the treatment. Heavy metals, such as lead, zinc, and cadmium, may remain in the water and create problems of pollution. The wastewater may also contain complex molecules, including pesticides and hormones that may harm the animals that drink it. These residues are a source of great concern, especially in situations where water has to be used many times, that these compounds can accumulate in drinking water and affect human populations.

The other means by which elements move along the pathway from a living to a nonliving form is by death. There are two main methods for the disposal of human remains, burial and burning. In burial, decomposition releases the elements contained in the body and these enter the soil. In most cases, however, the release takes place at a depth that is considerably below the rooting level of plants, so the elements are not immediately available for cycling back through the living organisms. Even if this were possible, however, the local habitat in which corpses are interred (a graveyard) would provide few opportunities for movement of elements back into the main nutrient cycle of the city ecosystem. It is notable that many cultures employ techniques of embalming or mummification, which seek to reduce the pace of decomposition. The outcome is that the cemetery is not an important part of nutrient cycling for the city ecosystem. Incineration of bodies by cremation is becoming increasingly favored as space becomes scarce in the city. Burning organic tissues at high temperature releases some elements into the atmosphere, while others remain as ash. Carbon, of course, is released on combustion as carbon dioxide, and hydrogen and oxygen as water vapor. Nitrogen and sulfur, mainly contained in proteins, are also released into the atmosphere as oxides of these elements. Potassium is partly converted to gaseous oxides, but some remains in the ash. Calcium, magnesium, and phosphorus are largely left in the ash. Disposal of these elements depends upon the wishes of relatives of the dead person, but it is unlikely that the elements will reenter the cycle of the city. Some ashes may be transported to rural areas, either terrestrial or aquatic, and dispersed there, in which case the elements can become available once again for the next great cycle.

Other cycles in the city

Although humans dominate the food web of the city, there are other cycles of elements that need to be considered. The automobile itself behaves almost like an independent organism, demanding gasoline for its energy supply and generating waste products in its operation. Industrial activities involve the import of raw materials to the city that are then exported in a new form, often with the production of waste products in the process. Humans themselves also use a whole range of materials that are not actually essential to the maintenance of their lives but are convenient for packaging foods or other consumer products. Many of these materials are of short-term use, so they become added to the waste output of the city. Industry often needs to import raw materials. Some of these are exported once more in the form of manufactured products, but some waste is usually generated and must be discharged by the city. We can think of the city, therefore, as a gigantic organism. It consumes food and raw materials that it obtains from its surroundings (usually referred to as its hinterland); it uses the food and gasoline for the combined respiration of its inhabitants and their cars; and it produces unwanted waste materials that it casts back into its environment.

The atmosphere provides a very convenient means of waste disposal. The movement of air as winds pass over and through the city causes a constant replacement of the oxygen that we need (both for ourselves and for the combustion of fuel). It also allows us to release waste gases, secure in the knowledge that they will be transported out of our immediate environment. Carbon dioxide is the most obvious product of the respiring city, and this can build up in our houses, offices, streets, and classrooms. Ventilation allows it to escape into the city atmosphere and to be carried out into the surrounding countryside. Carbon dioxide is toxic in high concentrations, but it is fortunately not a major constituent of the atmosphere, being present at between 0.03 and 0.04 percent by volume of the atmosphere. Although toxic to us, it is vital to green plants, which take in the gas from the atmosphere and convert it to sugars using the energy from sunlight (the process of photosynthesis). The production of waste carbon dioxide by cities and its dispersal into the countryside, therefore, might be regarded as a good thing because it provides more of the gas for green plants to use. In part this is true. Raising the level of carbon dioxide in the atmosphere does cause plants to grow faster, but on a global scale it can also have a harmful effect. Carbon dioxide, along with water vapor and several other gases, does not absorb visible light, which passes through unaffected; but this gas does absorb heat energy. Light from the Sun passes through the atmosphere, but when it reaches the surface of the Earth it is absorbed and converted into heat. When this heat is radiated from the ground, it becomes absorbed by gases like carbon dioxide in the atmosphere and does not escape back into space. In many ways this process resembles the working of a greenhouse, in which glass allows light energy in but prevents heat from escaping. For this reason, gases that act in this way are called *greenhouse gases* and the overall process the *greenhouse effect*. The excessive production of carbon dioxide by our cities and, to some extent, by mechanized agriculture is creating a global problem by resulting in the retention of heat in the atmosphere and causing a gradual rise in the Earth's temperature. As climate changes, the alteration will have an effect both on our cities and on our agriculture (see "Climate change," pages 189–192). Meanwhile, if we wish to avoid the problems of climate change, we need to cut down on carbon emissions by looking for alternative energy sources rather than fossil fuels.

Carbon is not the only element that we discharge into the atmosphere of our cities. There are other elements within fossil fuels that are converted into gases when we combust them. Sulfur and nitrogen are the two main elements that we cast into the atmosphere when we burn organic matter, both being released as oxides. Globally, we release about 80 million tons of sulfur into the atmosphere each year by burning fossil fuels. This is about 10 times the amount released naturally from volcanoes. The most common form of this discharged sulfur is the gas sulfur dioxide. This compound dissolves in water and becomes further oxidized to produce sulfuric acid, so the consequence of our releasing this gas into the atmosphere is that we turn the rain acid.

Nitrogen is also released from organic materials (including fossil fuels) by combustion and, like sulfur, is discharged in the form of oxides. Like the oxides of sulfur, these oxides of nitrogen dissolve in water to produce an acid, nitric acid, which adds to the acidity of the rain. Around 3 million tons of nitrogen are released into the atmosphere each year in this form as a result of human activity. One of the most common oxides of nitrogen, nitrous oxide, also acts as a greenhouse gas and contributes to the climate change problem.

Acid rain is therefore one of the major and unwanted exports from our industrial cities. The acidity has direct harmful consequences on our buildings, eroding stone surfaces, especially limestone. It also has a direct impact on plants, stripping off the protective wax layer that covers their leaves and exposing them to desiccation and to infection by microbes. Some organisms are very sensitive to acidity, including many of the mosses and lichens that are found on trees and on buildings, even in cities. The increase in the acidity of rainfall over the last 150 years has resulted in the loss of these plants from inner city areas and from the regions downwind of industrial activity. Just as plants are damaged by these pollutants and the resultant acidity, so are we. Our lungs find it difficult to cope with high levels of acidity and this can cause many respiratory problems, such as asthma and bronchitis. In serious cases the disease emphysema can result, which causes a loss of elasticity in the lungs and blocks the air sacs through which we absorb oxygen. It can prove fatal.

Our activities in the cities, especially the use of automobiles, trucks, and buses, also generate particulate pollutants. These are tiny fragments of solid matter, including ash, dust, smoke, and pollen from our city plants. Some of these can produce respiratory problems, such as asthma and bronchitis, in humans. About a quarter of the particulate pollutants found in cities is derived from the exhaust fumes of motor vehicles, and a further quarter from industrial activities, mining, and construction works. Much of the remainder comes from other forms of combustion, such as energy production in power stations and also domestic sources, such as cigarette smoking. Biological particles, including pollen, bacteria, and viruses, compose about 10 percent of the total load of particulates in the city atmosphere. The effect of particulates on the human respiratory system depends on the size of these different particles. Larger particles are filtered in the nasal passages and become trapped in mucus. But finer particles, especially the group known as PM10s, can penetrate into the lung where they may damage the lining. PM10 refers to particulate matter smaller than 10 microns in diameter; a micron is a thousandth of a millimeter. One important source of PM10s is exhaust produced by an inefficient diesel engine.

Air pollution resulting from motor exhausts and individual human activity, such as smoking, tend to accumulate close to the ground. The canyon effect of city streets (see "The microclimate of cities," pages 19–26) encourages the formation of still air in the protected lower regions of the city canyon. In the case of industrially produced pollutants, we make efforts to remove them from our immediate neighborhood by forcing them high into the atmosphere, using tall chimneys, and dispersing them. But by doing so the city is only exporting its waste to other ecosystems, both natural ones and the agricultural ecosystem from which it derives its own food. The gases that harm living plants in the city also damage the crops that grow in the countryside, so dispersing pollutants does not actually solve the problem. Sometimes we succeed in sending the pollutants over national boundaries. The industrial regions of the northeastern United States export some of their aerial pollutants to Canada, and the northwestern countries of Europe, including Britain, Germany, and Poland, export theirs to Scandinavia. But to be solved rather than merely displaced, the problem of pollution needs to be considered on a global rather than a national scale, and it needs to be solved at the source. Low-sulfur coal can be burned instead of high-sulfur forms, such as lignite. Oil generally contains less sulfur than coal, so this may be preferable. Scrubbing the waste gases, that is, cleaning them before emission by passing them over absorptive materials or through water, can remove many of the offending substances. Taxation by government is usually an effective way of ensuring that industry adopts cleaner practices.

There is one other important waste gas that is generated in our cities and is often exported to the countryside, namely ozone. Ozone is chemically closely related to oxygen, but instead of having two atoms of oxygen in its molecule, it has three. This makes it a highly reactive substance. Because of its reactivity, ozone can damage plant tissues, by destroying chlorophyll, and can seriously damage lung tissue. It is generated by a complex series of reactions resulting from automobile emissions interacting with sunlight, so it is particularly common in cities with heavy motor traffic combined with bright sunlight. The photochemical smogs of Los Angeles, California, are produced because this city has precisely the conditions under which ozone is generated, but many other cities around the world suffer the same problem. Like sulfur and nitrogen oxides, ozone moves out of the city under the influence of winds and into the countryside, where it is even more harmful to agriculture than the acid-forming gases. The concentrations of ozone received by crops, such as beans, wheat, peanuts, and cotton, growing downwind of a city can reduce their yield by between 10 and 20 percent, even if they are only exposed for as little as seven hours.

The production of gaseous waste products by cities, therefore, represents a serious threat to the agricultural ecosystems that support them. Like natural ecosystems that become adjusted to changing conditions, our cities need to modify their waste outputs to avoid damaging their own sources of food and raw materials.

Waste disposal

The atmosphere is not the only medium by which the city can dispose of its waste materials. As already observed, water leaving the city can supply a convenient way of removing sewage, containing the unused organic matter and the surplus elements, such as nitrogen and phosphorus, from our bodies. Cities have long used (or misused) water in this way. Even ancient Rome had a massive sewer, the Cloaca Maxima, leading waste into the Tiber River. Water has often been used for the disposal of other forms of waste, too, such as industrial effluent. The sediments of Lake Washington in Seattle, for example, reveal the history of waste discharge into this natural ecosystem. Before 1890 the sediments of the lake contained only very small quantities of lead, derived from the erosion of local rocks and soil that were not rich in this metal. By the 1970s the sediments contained around 20 times the natural concentration of lead, caused by the growth of industry in the region and the casual discharge of lead-containing waste into the water supplies to the lake. Much of the waste was probably in the form of dust that was blown by the wind and then washed into the lake.

Lead is a toxic material that accumulates in the body, so its presence in the dust, soil, and water of cities is a matter for concern. It was once a major component of paints and was

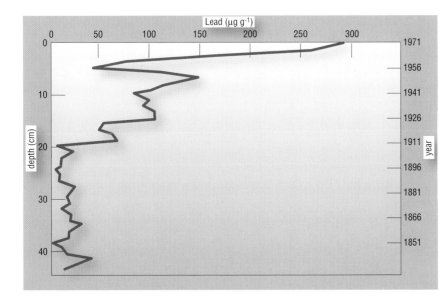

The concentration of lead (Pb) in the sediments of Lake Washington, near Seattle. There is a strong increase in lead concentrations in the upper layers of sediments. Additional lead has been released into the lake as a pollutant in the 20th century, reflecting the growth of the city of Seattle.

added to gasoline to improve engine performance, and these sources of the element have resulted in extensive pollution of our cities. Children in poor neighborhoods are especially at risk of lead exposure from dust and old paintwork, and this contamination could prove harmful to their development.

Mercury is another poisonous element that is produced as a waste product in many industrial processes. At one time it was used in agriculture as a seed dressing to prevent fungal infections of the seed, but its impact on bird populations and its implication in human deaths in the 1950s led people to avoid using it in this role. Mercury has also been extensively used in paper manufacture and this has led to pollution problems in countries such as Canada and Japan. Again, one can gain an impression of the rising scale of pollution by analyzing the sediments of lakes and oceans affected by our major cities. In the Santa Barbara Basin of California, for example, the concentration of mercury in sediments is now five times greater than in preindustrial times.

Both lead and mercury are examples of heavy metals, most of which are accumulative poisons in animals, including humans. Our bodies protect themselves to some extent and eliminate much of these toxins that enter our bloodstream. But this also creates a problem because it means that our excreted waste is also rich in heavy metals, thus contaminating sewage. As was already explained, sewage treatment does not normally remove these waste products, so they remain in discharged water and in solid effluent, presenting a health risk if treated human excrement is used as agricultural fertilizer. So the "recycling" of human waste through the agricultural ecosystem must be approached with care. Nonetheless, recycling as a general approach to element use in the city is clearly an important one. If we recover and remove more of the materials we use in the city, then it will cut down on our demands for natural resources (such as water, oil, metals, and so on) and will reduce the problem of waste disposal that our cities generate.

What are the alternatives to disposing waste products into rivers? Incineration is one commonly used method. But this may result in harmful materials being cast into the atmosphere rather than into water, so it is not entirely satisfactory.

Landfill involves the burying of waste in the ground, and this is still very widely used throughout the world. Holes in the ground, however, are not very common, and only certain types of holes are suitable for waste disposal. Buried waste decomposes, and harmful components, such as chemical toxins and heavy metals, will leak out of the burial site into subterranean water, possibly finding their way into human water supplies. The landfill site, therefore, must be geologically secure so that no leakage can take place, and this is a requirement that is often difficult to achieve. Even if a suitable location is found, the decay of buried, compacted organic materials deprived of atmospheric oxygen can lead to the formation of methane gas. Methane is highly inflammable, so its production creates a safety hazard, but it is also a very serious greenhouse gas, and its leakage to the atmosphere is

Garbage tractor and seagulls on a sunny day at the dump. Landfill as a means of garbage disposal is still widely used, but eventually there will be no more sites for waste dumping. (Courtesy of Erin Walsh)

even more harmful than that of carbon dioxide. Getting rid of the waste products of our cities will continue to test the ingenuity of humankind over the coming years.

Conclusions

Although the word *ecosystem* is usually used to describe natural habitats, both the farm and the city can be considered ecosystems, and this approach can help us to understand how they function. Ecosystems are characterized by a flow of energy through them and a cycling of materials within them. Both farms and cities depend upon supplies of energy, both in the form of natural sunlight (essential for crop photosynthesis) and in other forms, mainly derived from fossil fuels but also from other sources, including hydro, solar, wind, and so on. Farms need these additional sources of energy because they are used to produce artificial fertilizers and pesticides, and they power the machinery used in plowing, irrigation, harvesting, and transport of products. Cities need extra energy for lighting, heating, transport, and industry.

Farms and cities also cycle materials within themselves, using and reusing the elements needed for life and for industry. Just like natural ecosystems, farms and cities interact with one another and exchange energy and materials. The main flow of energy and nutrient elements is from farm to city, where the higher density of the human population requires a food supply. Farms are able to recycle some of the elements, such as by using animal dung as fertilizer, but cities generate large quantities of waste that has to be exported. It is possible to construct energy and nutrient budgets for the farm and the city in precisely the same way as for natural ecosystems. These will help us to understand how we can best balance energy flow and element cycling both within and between agricultural and urban areas.

CHAPTER 4

BIODIVERSITY IN FARMS AND CITIES

The most obvious plants and animals of our created and managed environment are those that we have deliberately installed there. Our fields are filled with our chosen plants, whether corn or wheat, sugarcane or bananas. Each part of the world is fitted out with the crop species and variety best suited to the particular climate and soil conditions that prevail there. Trees, grown for fruit crops or for timber, for cork or for rubber, are taken around the world and established where conditions allow, and these are grown generally in one-species assemblages sometimes referred to as *monocultures.* Similarly, we have chosen a number of animal species that supply our needs (cattle and sheep, goats and pigs) and have taken these to different parts of the world where we have created or adapted the environments they require for success. In our agriculture, therefore, we have taken natural habitats and simplified them in terms of biological diversity, or *biodiversity,* just as we have simplified the energy flow patterns of the original ecosystems (see "Energy flow in farms," pages 66–69).

But does agriculture necessarily mean low diversity? It is tempting to regard the human-created ecosystems of farms and cities as wildlife deserts, but this is actually far from true. Over the course of 10,000 years, people have created new ranges of habitats in almost all parts of the world as we have constructed our farmlands and towns. Many of the plants and animals already resident in the areas we have cultivated and settled in have been sufficiently adaptable to take advantage of new opportunities presented to them by our activities. Others have traveled around the world, often with our help, to take up residence in the areas we have settled. Some of these have been entirely harmless from the point of view of our welfare. Both the American robin on our lawns and the mockingbird on the telephone wires have used the habitats we have created, but they present no threat to our well being. Indeed, they even add to the attractiveness of our homes and gardens. But the rats in our sewers and the ants in our kitchens, though equally proficient at making a living in the new conditions we have set up, steal our food supplies and contaminate what they do not steal, so we are unwilling to share our habitat with them.

When we create arable fields with plowed soils and a regular pattern of planting and harvest, and when we clear forest to establish meadows where we can graze our cattle, we are actually reversing the natural pattern of vegetation development. In the natural course of vegetation establishment, called *succession,* less complex systems develop over time into more complex ones. Agriculture involves a reversal of this process and complex natural ecosystems are converted into simple agricultural ones. When we develop arable agriculture in the prairie regions, for example, grassland is converted to an area of disturbed soil, reversing the normal course of vegetation development. In those temperate regions of the world where forests form the natural vegetation, the establishment of farms involves a reduction in the total biomass of the ecosystem. Trees are removed and herbaceous plants are encouraged, either by planting or by grazing. When agricultural land is abandoned, however, the natural development of succession resumes with the invasion of coarse perennial herbs, shrubs, and eventually trees, until the forest is healed over once more. This process is often called "old field succession" and it is characteristic of many neglected areas of land in the eastern United States. In reversing the course of succession as we create fields, we also provide opportunities for the native animals and plants adapted to the early stages of colonization to become established. A new set of species, not normally present in the mature forest, prevails under the conditions we have created.

In general, more advanced stages of a succession contain more species than earlier stages; mature woodland contains more species than an area of scrub or of grassland. But the nature of our settlement and farming is such that we have often created a mosaic pattern in our landscape, with patches of arable land being mixed with grassland areas and with residual patches of woodland. Highways often have uncultivated strips of grassland running along their sides, and occasional human settlements create oases of ornamental gardens, tree plantations, water features, and many other microhabitats. This means that the *cultural landscape* (that is, the landscape in which human activity has had an extensive influence) may actually be more diverse than the natural landscape. This should not come as a surprise to anyone who has walked through dense natural forests and who also has experience of rural or suburban human habitats. In a natural forest, people are likely to see fewer species and fewer overall numbers of birds, butterflies, and wildflowers in an hour's walk than if they spent the same time in an area of suburban gardens or in an area of patchy, diverse farmland. In both tropical and temperate areas, statistical analyses have shown that increased numbers of people results in increased numbers of plant and animal species. There is a limit to this correlation, of course. When human population density becomes extremely high, there is no room for other species.

Ecologists have set up a simple rule called the *intermediate disturbance hypothesis*. This is a rather grand title for the idea explored here, that a degree of disturbance in a habitat (by humans or by any other factor) can lead to an increase in the general level of diversity. The use of the word *intermediate* here implies that we can have too much of a good thing, and this is indeed true. If the degree of disturbance continues to increase, producing a concrete jungle in our cities and areas of uniform, uninterrupted arable fields in our countryside, then habitat and species diversity inevitably diminish. According to the principle of intermediate disturbance, there is an optimal level of habitat modification that can diversify the environment and open up new opportunities without involving the loss of too many species. The general effects of disturbance and habitat fragmentation, however, will inevitably result in the loss of some species. In the case of forest clearance for settlement and agriculture, these will usually be the species of old-growth forest, or ancient undisturbed forest. The forest species, and there are many, that are contented with open glades and forest edges (including many bird and deer species, for example) may well be favored by the development of a cultural landscape.

Domesticated plants and animals

The most evident plants and animals of the agricultural ecosystems are those that we have placed there. The whole ecosystem is managed with them in mind. What is strikingly obvious about our domesticated plants and animals is that there are precious few of them.

Take the plants that we use as the basis for our food production. The table on page 107 shows the approximate global production of the most important plant species. It is immediately apparent that just three species of plants (wheat, corn [maize], and rice) dominate the world's food production. In fact, these three species between them produce about half of the plant food products of the world. Among the remaining species, there is a rapid decline in production from the more important

Stalk of wheat. This plant species (Triticum aestivum) *is responsible for more than 17 percent of the world's human food production.* (Courtesy of Fogstock)

to the less important species. Just 15 species of plants are responsible for 96 percent of the agricultural plant production of the Earth. Considering how many plants are available on this planet (about 300,000 vascular plant species; that is, flowering plants, conifers, and ferns), this is an extraordinarily narrow range upon which to base the survival of the human species. On the other hand, it does say much for these select few species that they have been able to support global human populations for so long and so successfully.

Contributions of different crop species to global food production by plants

Crop species	Percentage of global plant food production
Wheat	17.4
Corn (maize)	17.3
Rice	17.0
Potatoes	8.7
Sugar beet	7.5
Cassava	4.8
Barley	4.5
Sweet potatoes	3.9
Soybeans	3.9
Oil palm fruit	2.7
Tomatoes	2.6
Sorghum	2.0
Oranges	1.5
Cabbages	1.5
Coconuts	0.9
Plantains	0.8
Beans	0.5
Carrots	0.5
Peppers	0.4
Lettuce	0.4
Chickpeas	0.2
Lentils	0.1

Another constraint on the biodiversity of domesticated plants is the fact that each of these plant species is usually grown in a single-species population, a monoculture. This makes sense to the agriculturalist because such an arrangement is easier to manage. We can sow the seeds at one time, apply the appropriate fertilizers in the right quantity, use the same pest control methods, and harvest the crop using one set of machinery. Imagine how difficult harvesting would be if apple trees were grown scattered in a wheat field. So monoculture makes practical sense, but it is not what would be found in a natural ecosystem, where there are usually many different species of plants growing together, each tapping the resources of the environment in a different way. They may grow at different heights and take light at different levels and intensities; they may root in different horizons of the soil; they may flower and release seed at different times, so that their demands for nutrients and water do not coincide. In the case of a monoculture, all individual plants are trying to do the same job in precisely the same way and all at the same time. This creates a high level of competition, which could result in some resources being in short supply at one time and present in excess at another time of year. In addition, the growth of monocultures leaves a crop exposed to the problem of an epidemic spread of pests and diseases. An insect that normally has to hunt around in a diverse plant community for the species it requires for egg laying finds it very easily if it grows in extensive single-species plantations.

Some agricultural systems attempt to use a more ecologically sound approach by growing a number of compatible crops together. In Egypt, for example, a combination of date palms, citrus trees, and beans is sometimes grown in the same field and at the same time. The palms are tall but cast little shade, so orange or lemon trees can be grown beneath them. The patches of open ground between the trees will then support a bean crop, which, in addition to supplying beans, fixes nitrogen in its roots, thus adding to the fertility of the soil. Although successful for relatively small farming operations, this style of agriculture clearly cannot be adopted for all crops in all parts of the world. Our wheat and corn will continue to be grown in extensive monocultures for the foreseeable future.

We also exploit animals for food, and it has been estimated that there are as many head of domestic livestock on the

Earth as there are human beings. Among these, just two species, cow and sheep, account for around two-thirds the total number. Pig, goat, and water buffalo follow some distance behind, and the remaining main domestic livestock (horse, ass, and mule) are usually used for their work output rather than their food value. We eat animals because they are a richer source of protein than plant material. Although meat represents only about 10 percent of our total energy intake, it accounts for about 33 percent of the protein in our diet. Some of the constituent building blocks of proteins (amino acids) are almost totally restricted to animal sources. As explained in chapter 3, eating animals is energetically inefficient because so much energy goes to waste each time it is transferred from one feeding level to another. By eating a grazing animal, such as a sheep, we take in only about 10 percent of the energy that was present in the grass the animal ate. But, on the other hand, we cannot eat grass. The herds of

A flock of sheep. Sheep and cattle together account for two-thirds of the animal food production for people. (Courtesy of Fogstock)

domestic grazers that roam our pastoral landscapes eat about four times as much vegetable material as the entire human race, but much of this food would not be suitable for human consumption, so the sheep gives us a way of harvesting at least some of this available energy. The system becomes very inefficient in energy terms when we take plant food that would be suitable for humans, such as corn, and feed it to cattle.

The lack of diversity that is apparent in domesticated plants is even more marked in the case of domesticated animals. We seem to have made virtually no advances in this field for the last 8,000 years. Only in very recent times have there been attempts to broaden the base of our animal diet by farming animals that we have previously neglected, such as salmon in the seas or game animals in the tropical savannas. We have been contented with our limited range of domestic herbivores because they have a very wide range of ecological tolerance and diet, coupled with a high genetic diversity that has allowed us to breed a considerable number of varieties, selected for specific sets of conditions.

African game animals are prepared to graze in a relatively limited number of habitats, however, compared with the wide ranges of domesticated herbivores. Only the elephant has a wide variety of potential habitats, and that is an animal unsuitable for domestication and harvesting because of its very slow reproductive rate. But some of these wild animals may have other advantages, for example, the capacity to survive drought or to resist the impact of some pest insects, such as tsetse fly. There are certainly opportunities to expand the number of animals we exploit as food resources and thus to increase the biodiversity of our pastoral ecosystems.

Making a living in farmland

The range of plants and animals other than the domesticated species that we find on farmlands can be divided into two broad biogeographical groups. There are the native species that existed in the region even before the arrival and expansion of human agricultural activities, and there are those that have arrived since, often as a result of transport by humans, either inadvertent or deliberate. This latter group may have come from far away, even from distant parts of the planet, and established themselves in the new conditions so conveniently created by the humans who transported them.

While these plants and animals are of interest to the ecologist or the biogeographer, the farmer has a rather different way of classifying the wild organisms of the farm: They are either harmful or harmless (some of the latter even attaining a helpful status). Any organism, plant, animal, or microbe that damages the productivity of the farm by reducing the health or performance of the domesticated plants and animals is regarded as a pest. A pest may be a predator, a parasite, or a competitor of the domesticated species, but whatever its mode of activity, the farmer would be pleased to be rid of it. Ever since the origins of agriculture, therefore, farmers have found themselves in direct conflict with pests. Even the first book of the Bible, which was probably first written down in Bronze Age times but is far more ancient, records farmers' frustration with pests: "cursed is the ground. Thorns and thistles shall it bring forth to thee. In the sweat of thy face shalt thou eat bread."

Weeds

The term that we would usually use for the "thorns and thistles" referred to in the biblical quotation is "weeds." Weeds are plant pests. There is no biological definition of a weed because the term is used only in connection with human attitudes. It is a plant that grows where humans do not wish it to grow. It gets in our way or interferes with our plans. We probably think of weeds as those irritating little plants that are constantly springing up in flower beds or those that can choke our agricultural crops, but weeds also include water plants that infest rivers and canals, affecting shipping, and trees that invade forestry plantations and compete with the timber-producing species. Wherever humans are creating habitats for their own pleasure or profit, there are plant species that exploit the new opportunities to their own advantage. It is natural that this should be the case because natural selection will always put pressure upon species to

A neglected field can become colonized by a wealth of weed species, as in the case of this field in northern Germany. (Courtesy of Peter D. Moore)

adapt to new sets of conditions. Weeds will always be on an evolutionary roller coaster.

Weeds have been with us ever since the origins of agriculture. Archaeological evidence from fossil plant remains show that crops of seeds have always been contaminated with plants that were not intended to be there, namely weeds. Although it is not possible to define a weed in precise biological terms, one can observe certain features that place particular plants in the weed category, characteristics that make them successful as colonizers and persistent inhabitants of arable fields. Obviously, not all weeds possess all of these features, but most possess at least some of them:

1. The plant can grow and produce seeds under a wide range of conditions.
2. It grows rapidly, reaching maturity and flowering early.
3. It can produce large numbers of seeds.
4. Seeds are adapted to both short- and long-distance dispersal.

5. Seeds germinate in a wide range of soil conditions.
6. Some seeds are able to remain dormant in the soil.
7. The plant is not dependent on special pollinators or seed dispersal agents.
8. It is capable of vegetative growth.
9. It can compete with other plant species.
10. Underground parts fragment easily to prevent removal.

Close examination of these points shows that they fall into two groups. The first seven points concern reproduction and seed characteristics, while the final three points are con-

Thistles rank among the worst of weeds. The creeping thistle (Cirsium arvense) *has underground stems and can also spread by means of abundant seed production.* (Courtesy of Mark Lane)

cerned with vegetative features (that is, those concerned with growth rather than reproduction). Annual weeds (those that complete their life cycle within the course of a single year) are very dependent on seed production, so the seven reproductive features apply particularly to them. Perennial weeds, on the other hand, are more often endowed with features that enhance their persistence and competition with the surrounding plants. Tall stems and robust growth, rapid extension by runners along the ground, and even the production of inhibitory chemicals to suppress the germination and growth of other species are among the armory of the typical perennial weed.

Weeds are among the most abundant plant species, but they have not always been so plentiful. It is possible to follow the history of weeds and their rise to success by tracing their fossil remains in archaeological strata and also preserved in the sediments of old lakes and peat bogs. The archaeological evidence is important because it confirms that weeds were associated with particular human cultures in the past. It can also sometimes help explain how weeds managed to move from one part of the world to another. In Europe around 2,000 years ago, for example, the Romans were extending their empire northward from the Mediterranean into the dense forests of uncivilized regions in what are now Germany, France, and Britain. They took with them many species of plants, some because they used them for food or for medicinal purposes and others simply by accident. Perhaps their seeds were mixed with food species or were present in soil carried large distances on boots and wagon wheels. When the Romans traveled north they took a plant called ground elder, or gout weed (*Aegopodium podagraria*). This is a perennial plant belonging to the carrot family and it was used for medicinal purposes; it was believed to cure gout, a condition in which the joints become painfully inflamed. The plant originated in western Asia, so it was well known to the Romans, who traded and conducted military activities in that region, but it did not occur in the north of Europe, so it had to be transported there. But gout weed proved to be a strong competitor with the native plants of the north. Its roots penetrate deep into the soil, perhaps as deep as 30 feet, so once established it is almost impossible to eradicate. It also grows in a dense mass, eliminating all other plants in its surroundings. What began as a valuable medicinal plant has become a weed, and it remains a problem right up to the present day.

Scientists know the story of gout weed because of its first occurrence in Roman archaeological levels; it is not present in earlier times. The Romans carried this plant deliberately, but other weeds transported by the Romans were probably accidental. For example, some types of poppy (*Papaver* species) and the scarlet pimpernel (*Anagallis arvensis*) are weeds of arable fields that were carried along the Roman roads into all parts the empire. In Britain alone there were around 6,500 miles of Roman road constructed between 78 and 400 C.E., so the increased movement of people that resulted from this communication system greatly assisted the spread of weeds. The scarlet pimpernel did not stop its spread after hitching a ride with the Romans; it has since managed to use human transport as a means of spreading all around the world, including North America.

Some weeds have left evidence of their spread by the pollen that they produced. Pollen is the means by which the male reproductive cells of the flowering plant are transported to the receptive but static female egg cells. These reproductive cells are fragile and are especially vulnerable to desiccation, so while traveling they are securely protected in a robust coat. This coat is so tough, in fact, that it survives as a fossil under certain conditions, particularly in the very wet conditions of lake sediments or in peat bogs, where decomposition is very slow. Many pollen grains can be identified in this fossil state, and the layered nature of lake sediments and peat provides a time sequence so that we can trace the history of the plants that produced them. The fossil pollen record is most complete for species that are pollinated by wind, because these species have to produce far more pollen than plants using insects for pollination, and the pollen grains are dispersed far and wide, some ending up on the surfaces of lakes and bogs. Ragweed (*Ambrosia* species) is a good example of such a plant. Today this is a serious weed of arable land in North America, but the pollen record in the lakes of the northeastern United States provides evidence that it has only recently become widespread. Disturbance of the original forest by Native American settlements produced clearings that soon recovered after they were abandoned when the farmers and hunters moved on, but the more permanent openings created by European settlers in the 18th and 19th centuries generated a more extensive weed flora, including ragweed, which has persisted ever since.

Historical records have also provided evidence of weeds spreading in more recent times. Take the pineapple weed (*Matricaria discoidea*), for instance. No one is quite sure of the origin of this plant (which incidentally gets its name because of the smell of its crushed foliage), but it is probably a native of Northeast Asia. Pineapple weed is a small, daisylike plant with feathery leaves that lacks the white ray florets of a daisy, so is really rather unattractive. By the early 19th century it had found its way to North America and was well established in Oregon. From there it continued its movements eastward, almost certainly being carried accidentally by people, and in 1871 it was first found in Britain. Over the next 50 years this plant became one of the most common wayside species throughout the temperate world. Its explosive success was almost certainly due to a new invention that human beings inadvertently placed at its disposal: the automobile. The highly sculptured surface of vehicle tires is ideal for trapping soil and mud, and the pineapple weed produces up to 450 seeds per flower head, which are easily carried in this way. In one experiment, the tires of a car were carefully cleaned, and the car was then driven for 65 miles along highways and tracks. The tires were then hosed and the dirt collected to check for seeds. A total of 220 seeds of pineapple weed germinated from this dirt when incubated in a sterile growth medium, proving the efficiency of the seed dispersal system. The remarkable success of this once restricted species is now understood.

Some weeds use water as a means of transport. The purple loosestrife (*Lythrum salicaria*) moved in the opposite direction from that of the pineapple weed, traveling west to the United States from Europe with the help of humans. People enjoyed its attractive flowers, so they brought it over to the

New World in the 1840s as a decorative plant. The map shows the spread of the plant through the United States and Canada. It had been present in the country for over 50 years before its range expansion began, and this westward movement was greatly assisted by the construction of the Erie Canal and the consequent increase in shipping. The purple loosestrife hitched a ride on water traffic and began to colonize the west.

Studies of the history of plant pests raise a persistent question: Where did they come from originally? What sort of habitat did these plants occupy before human beings gave them their great opportunity to become common? Where, for instance, were poppies and ragweed before people came along? One thing that most weeds have in common is that they like disturbed conditions. Before there were farmers to disturb the ground, they must have relied upon natural disturbances to provide the right sets of conditions. Forest fire, wind damage, floods, and erosion all created habitats in

The spread of the purple loosestrife (Lythrum salicaria) *through North America following its introduction from Europe in the 1840s. It has proved an invasive weed in wetland habitats.*

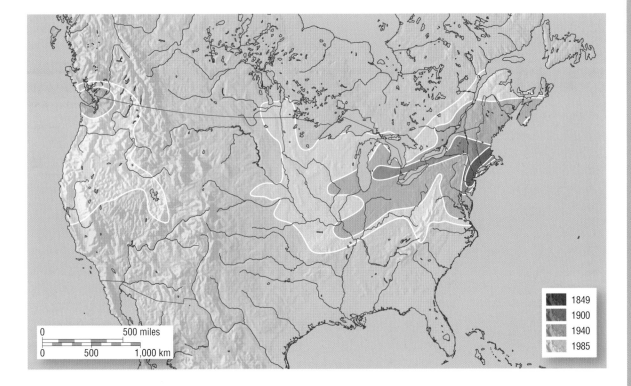

0 500 miles	■ 1849
0 500 1,000 km	■ 1900
	■ 1940
	■ 1985

which bare soil was exposed and where species of plant with the attributes we now associate with weeds would have been at home. Even the intense erosion resulting from glacial movements in mountainous areas may have produced appropriate conditions for potential weeds, once the glaciers had retreated and only the shattered rocks remained. It is interesting to note that some of the plants whose pollen is associated with the first impacts of agricultural people in fossil sediments are also to be found at the end of the last Ice Age, invading the bare soils left by the melting ice.

So there were suitable habitats for "weeds" even before people produced more extensive habitats, and the kinds of attributes needed in those disturbed habitats are precisely the qualities that subsequently made them into efficient weeds. Damaged gaps in a forest, for example, could be invaded only by plants with efficient means of long-distance dispersal, so plants with airborne seeds or seeds carried by birds or mammals that also use forest gaps would have possessed a means of invasion. Once present, their residence time was short. Damaged areas soon heal, making conditions too shaded once more, so a short lifespan and rapid production of large quantities of well-dispersed seeds were needed. But there is an alternative strategy. It is possible to stay in the same place in a dormant form and to wait until the next disturbance comes along, as it must in the course of time. This can also be achieved by means of the seed, for it can lie dormant until conditions wake it. Many weed seeds are capable of 100 years of dormancy, and it is possible that some may even survive for 400 years or longer. Within this time period it is entirely likely that a new catastrophe will have occurred and the weed's time will have come again. Some weed seeds have their dormancy broken by light, so when the soil is turned over (as when a tree is blown down or struck by lightning), the weed is activated once more.

Weeds may also have persisted in more permanent sites, such as the eroding banks of rivers, or on coastal sand dunes, prairies disturbed by the digging of badgers, or some of the unstable soils of dry regions. In any site where there is frequent catastrophic disturbance, plants will have evolved that are well equipped to take up the new challenges of the arable field or the urban garden. The weeds have always been out there waiting.

But why is it that a species may be unproblematic in its native country and yet may become a serious nuisance in an alien region? The purple loosestrife, for example, is a plant of marshes and riversides in Europe that causes no problems in its native continent. When introduced to North America, however, it proved aggressive and achieved a dominant status in many habitats, eliminating native species. The success of such species away from the original homes may be lack of natural deterrents: They leave their predators and parasites behind. The grazing insects, fungal pathogens, and viral diseases that attack such species in their homeland may not be transported or may not survive in the new location, so the invader becomes a pest.

The control of weeds by using chemical herbicides is often possible, but alternatives are available. One of these is biological control, or "biocontrol," the use of the plant's natural enemies for its control. In the western United States, for example, the tamarisk, or salt cedar tree (*Tamarix* species), is becoming a serious invasive weed of dry lands. Native to Europe and Asia, it was introduced as a windbreak and an ornamental plant in the 19th century. It may be possible to control its spread by introducing the Chinese leaf beetle (*Diorhabda elongate*), which attacks the plant's foliage. But first we must be quite sure that the beetle will only feed on the salt cedar, otherwise the intended control agent may turn into a worse pest than the plant it was brought to exterminate. The introduction of biocontrol agents must always be carried out with great care, particularly regarding the range of organisms they may begin to prey upon or parasitize.

Animal pests of farmland

The features that can make an animal into a pest species are rather different from those of a plant. Most agricultural weeds are pests because they compete with domestic plants for limited resources, such as light, water, mineral nutrients, or space. Animals, of course, occupy a different position in food webs, but some animal pests can behave in a similar way. Any animal that competes with our domestic herbivores for food, for example, is automatically a pest from the human point of view.

The European rabbit (*Oryctolagus cuniculus*) is a good example of a mammal that has competed with domestic herbivores and become a pest in many parts of the world. It came originally from Spain and the western Mediterranean and has been hunted since prehistoric times as a source of meat. The rabbit became semidomesticated as a result of human management of the colonies and was carried around Europe and established in warrens. These managed sets of burrows, often in sandy soils in dunes and heaths, provided a regular crop of animals for the pot. By 1,000 years ago the rabbit was widely spread through Europe, and it remains a pest in many regions, both because it eats crop plants and it consumes the grass that would otherwise be eaten by sheep and cattle. As a competitor with domestic grazers, however, it has proved most successful (or disastrous, according to your viewpoint) in Australia. It was deliberately introduced around 200 years ago, probably as a source of food, but became so widespread and abundant between 1900 and 1959 that it became the focus of major eradication campaigns, eventually leading to the use of a host-specific virus that proved highly contagious, causing a debilitating disease, myxomatosis. This virus was obtained from a South American forest rabbit in which the disease is nonfatal, but in the European rabbit, it caused 99.8 percent mortality. Amazingly, the rabbit has survived in Australia and is now genetically adapted to the virus, which in turn has become less virulent. European rabbits have been introduced into the United States but have not, in general, become a pest problem. They were introduced onto the San Juan Islands, off the coast of Washington, once more as a food resource, but there, too, they soon became highly destructive, in this case because of their habit of tunneling, which led to the collapse of some buildings.

What has made the European rabbit such a successful pest is its broad tolerance of different conditions (both climatic and soil) and its ability to breed rapidly. A female is able to produce as many as 30 young in a year, and although many of these will die early, this prodigious rate of reproduction enables the species to expand its population rapidly and to adapt genetically to new sets of conditions. There are many similarities, therefore, between the rabbit and the annual weed. Both have the capacity to breed rapidly and to thrive in a range of conditions. The European rabbit has also shown its ability to colonize habitats created by humans. Originating in warm temperate grasslands in Spain, it has proved capable of using the managed grasslands of pastoral farmland and has even been successful in exploiting lawns in suburban parks and gardens. In planting and managing areas of short turf, we have created exactly the conditions that the rabbit enjoys best.

Mammals are by no means the only pests to affect crop production; insects, on the whole, are even more important. No one knows how many species of insects there are in the world; some have estimated at about 8 million. They are a remarkably successful group that has evolved methods of tapping just about any source of food. Domesticated plants are a sitting target, being arranged in large populations of monocultures, just waiting to be consumed. Some insects attack the seeds before they have germinated. Others bore into stems or chew at the leaves or eat the flower bud. Still others attack the fruit as it forms, rendering it worthless as a harvestable crop. Some insects, such as the locust, will do all of these things at once, consuming the entire plant. It is clear that the farmer should be prepared to defend the crop from these insect pests with all possible weapons.

Pesticides are chemicals that are able to destroy the pest species; essentially, they are poisons. Some early pesticides used by farmers in the 19th century were cyanide and arsenic, which were very effective control agents against such insect pests as the cottony-cushion scale insect (*Icerya purchasi*) in California and the Colorado potato beetle (*Leptinotaras decemlineata*) in the eastern United States. But these materials are also highly poisonous to people, so the agricultural workers applying them were in danger of being poisoned in the process. Some more recent pesticides can be extremely powerful and yet appear to be less toxic to people, such as the compound DDT, which had an enormous impact on pest control when it was first used in the World War II. At that time DDT was used mainly to kill insects that carried diseases, such as mosquitoes and lice, but after the war it was also used on crops. It was not until 1954 that the side effects on other wildlife began to show. Fish began to be poisoned, together with their predators, such as grebes and herons. It became evident that the compound was not eliminated from the bodies of vertebrate animals but was accumulated in their fat deposits, eventually proving lethal. DDT was found to persist in the fatty milk of cattle, and hence it was present in the human food chain. Even the breast milk of nursing mothers was found to contain the toxin, and the chemical had spread so insidiously around the world that it was discovered even in the fat deposits of Antarctic penguins. As a result of these discoveries and concerns about the harmful effects on wildlife and humans, DDT was banned, as were various other toxins that had been previously accepted as harmless, such as the organophosphorus nerve poisons.

Plants have long faced the challenge of discouraging insect attackers, and many have developed defense chemicals that are much more specific than the chemical pesticides invented by humans. Pyrethrum, for example, is a chemical produced by a chrysanthemum species (*Chrysanthemum ariaefolium*), and it is very effective in paralyzing insects on contact. It does not seem to have any adverse effect on plants, so it can be safely used on crops, and its toxicity to mammals and birds is low. The search for more efficient and safe pesticides will continue, but plant-based "natural" insecticides may prove important in helping to find the ideal pesticide.

There are other ways of tackling the insect pest problem, for example, by using biological control agents such as predators or parasites of the offending insect. These methods have sometimes proved successful, especially in the case of pests transferred beyond their normal geographic range, which have thus escaped from their natural predators and parasites. Reuniting them with their old enemies is sometimes effective in controlling their populations. A more subtle method involves interrupting the life cycle of the insect by sterilizing males and releasing them in large numbers. This has been applied to the screwworm fly (*Cochliomyia hominivorax*), which invades the southern United States from Mexico each year. Irradiating captive male flies damages their reproductive organs so that they become sterile but are still able to mate. When released, they compete with fertile males and mate with the females but fail to fertilize them. So no fertile eggs are laid as a consequence of this coupling. The results of this program have varied over the years, but it is generally regarded as successful. An even more deceptive method is to use the same chemicals that the females of certain insects emit to attract males. These chemicals, called pheromones, are used to bait traps, which attract males that can subsequently be killed. Some moths have very powerful scent attractants of this type.

The control of insect pests is a complex area of research in which no two insects behave in the same way, so specific programs need to be established for each individual pest. Often a range of methods has to be applied together; this joint application is called "integrated pest management."

Microbial pests on the farm

Bacteria and fungi, together with viruses, are a threat not only to our own health but also to that of our domestic animals and plants. These organisms, like insect pests, are able to achieve rapid spread when their hosts are densely crowded, so control can be difficult. The consequences of the outbreak of disease in our food organisms can be catastrophic for human populations, as in the case of the great potato famine of Ireland in the 19th century. The potato was the staple diet of the Irish people at that time, so the outbreak of a fungal disease that destroys the young plant led to widespread starvation. Large-scale immigration of Irish people to the United States in the 19th century was mainly a consequence of the outbreak of disease in the potato crop; clearly, a microbial pest can alter the pattern of human settlement on the Earth.

One of the most serious diseases of wheat in the past has been the rust fungus *Puccinia graminis*. As its name implies, the rust fungus produces rusty spots over the leaves, causing a heavy loss in plant productivity. It is an unusual fungus because it has two hosts, the wheat plant (*Triticum aestivum*) and the barberry (*Berberis vulgaris*). Generally it spends its summer infesting wheat in the northerly areas, and then spends its winter on the barberry in the south. Each spring, therefore, clouds of windborne spores are carried northward where they invade the growing wheat crop. One obvious method of control is to eliminate the wild barberry plants. Although total destruction of the barberry has not been achieved, it has certainly become a rarer plant as a result of control measures.

The control of fungal diseases of crops has often involved the use of highly toxic chemicals. In the French countryside near Bordeaux, fungal infection of fruit trees first led to the use of copper sulfate as means of control, and it proved very successful. But this compound is poisonous to humans, so its use can have unexpected and unforeseen consequences, including the poisoning of people and domestic animals. Mercury compounds have been used to prevent fungal infection of seeds right up until the mid-20th century. The "Silent Spring" of the 1950s, when many songbirds perished, was partly caused by these highly toxic seed dressings, which resulted in the death of millions of birds. Like biocontrol, the management of microbial pests can create new problems.

One surprising outcome of sulfur dioxide pollution from the burning of fossil fuels has been the reduction of many fungal diseases in areas where air pollution is high. The black-spot disease of roses in gardens, for example, became much rarer as a result of high atmospheric sulfur. One of the unfortunate consequences of reducing sulfur pollution has been the return of black-spot disease.

Some diseases of domesticated animals have been controlled mainly by a policy of slaughter to avoid the further spread of an infection. Foot-and-mouth disease affects a number of domestic stock and has the capacity to travel rapidly from one area to another. The method by which it spreads is still uncertain, perhaps by human or vehicle transport in mud and dust, perhaps by birds flying from one farm to another, or perhaps simply carried through the air. Outbreaks of this disease are usually treated by strict quarantine, intended to avoid physical movement, and the destruction of all susceptible animals in the vicinity, to create a disease-free zone around the site of infection. The approach may seem wasteful of animal life, but eradication is still regarded as preferable to immunization, which effectively accepts that the disease becomes endemic at low levels in the domestic population.

Some microbial pests of domestic plants and animals can have direct impact on humans. In the cereal rye, for example, one fungus, called ergot (*Claviceps purpurea*), causes the development of black, enlarged swellings in the ear of the plant. These sclerotia are poisonous to humans, and their consumption, resulting from the contamination of flour with ergot, can prove fatal. The symptoms are twitching and shaking of the limbs, eventually leading to convulsions. In some cases, gangrene sets in (death of tissues due to disrupted blood circulation), and this may lead to the loss of fingers and even limbs prior to death. A recent fear has been the spread of a disease of the brain and spinal cord of cows, called bovine spongiform encephalopathy (BSE), into the human population, where it causes a similar disease, Creutzfeldt-Jakob disease (CJD). The disease seems to be contracted as a result of eating infected material from these tissues. There is no evidence that the muscle tissues, which are the main source of beef, can be infected, but the presence of this disease in cattle has caused grave concerns.

Inevitably, crop and animal husbandry present opportunities for the spread of disease, and the diversity of diseases is greater in warmer, tropical climates. If the climate of the world continues to become warmer, then the incidence and importance of disease in the agriculture of the temperate zone will undoubtedly rise.

Fortunately, the biodiversity of farmland is not entirely a consequence of the presence of pests. Many species of plants, insects, birds, and mammals have benefited from the development of arable and pastoral landscapes, and only a small proportion can be regarded as pests. Some are actually beneficial to the farmer, and others are, at worst, neutral to agricultural interests. Uncultivated areas in farmland are often regarded as a source of pests and weeds, but these same areas also contain many of the organisms that control pests, predatory insects, mammals, and birds. The farmer whose land contains these refuges for wildlife will find that the biodiversity they encourage is generally an advantage rather than the reverse.

As discussed earlier, the development of farmland often creates a mosaic landscape, where patches of arable land are mixed with woodland, grassland, roadside verge, and hedges (see "Patterns of development," pages 11–15). This varied landscape tends to support or even increase local biodiversity. Many butterflies find advantages in a diverse mixture of habitats, as do many bird species, including meadowlarks and bluebirds. Some insects and birds even feed upon the weed species of neglected land, for instance, the monarch butterfly (*Danaus plexipus*), whose caterpillars consume milkweed along the disturbed edges of highways, and goldfinches (genus *Carduelis*), which eat the seeds of many weeds. The roads are dangerous to wildlife, of course, and many insects, birds, and mammals die in collisions. But they, too, provide a resource that other organisms feed upon. Crows and magpies find roadsides a rich source of carrion, and starlings will collect in parking lots to gather insects from radiator grilles, usually served fresh and hot, ready for consumption. Although some plants and animals are lost in the fragmentation of the countryside, many more are favored.

Opportunities in the city

Just like farmland, the city can be a very diverse type of environment. It is patchy and fragmented, but it is also quite varied. Cities are often arranged in a series of roughly concentric zones (see the figure on page 16) and the opportunities for wildlife, both animal and plant, differ in each of these zones.

The central regions of cities (Zone A), where the business and commerce is mainly located, is also an area where money is often invested in supplying recreational areas for the workers, shoppers, and tourists. Extensive parks are often present, such as Central Park in New York and Hyde Park in London, England, where habitats include trees, grassland, and lakes. These parks provide limited but important rural conditions that will supply the needs of a wide range of plant and animal species. Since the vegetation is usually carefully managed, the opportunities for plant invasion may be limited, but animals, from earthworms to birds and mammals, often succeed in establishing themselves in the urban park. Red foxes (*Vulpes vulpes*) now abound in central London, England, and squirrels, particularly the eastern gray squirrel (*Sciurus carolinensis*), is a frequent sight in the eastern United States, as well as in many of the cities of Britain, where it has been introduced.

The buildings and streets of the inner city, as well as those of the next zone out (Zone B), consist of factories for light industries and residential tenement buildings, which present fewer opportunities for wildlife than the parks of the central area. There is little soil available for colonization, apart from the temporarily exposed soils in areas of demolition and reconstruction. There are some habitats that can be occupied, however. Even on the flat surfaces of bricks and concrete, some plants can establish themselves. Two types of moss often found in such locations are the wall screw moss (genus *Tortula*) and the cushion moss (genus *Grimmia*). Both of these form compact cushions on the tops of walls and have a dark

The moss Tortula muralis *growing on the top of a wall. The cushion form and the fine hair points on the leaves of the moss help to reduce evaporation, which is important for a plant living in a very dry environment.* (Courtesy of Peter D. Moore)

greenish color, often made gray by the presence of fine white hairs at the tip of each leaf. When they are dry, which is the case most of the time, the short stems of the screw moss coil like corkscrews and the hairs wrap around the stems to prevent total desiccation. The whiteness of the hairs may also serve to reflect some of the sunlight so that the plants do not become overheated. The mosses are able to survive in this dry state almost indefinitely; dried specimens stored in museums have been wetted after 100 years of drought and have instantly opened out, turned green, and begun to actively photosynthesize. This is a remarkable property of some mosses: the ability to become totally dry and to survive for very long periods. Equally remarkable is the rapid recovery; a moss cushion in a rain shower changes color before your eyes and begins to function once again. They may look delicate, but these mosses are among the toughest of plants when it comes to survival in the city.

Lichens are also capable of long-term survival in the drought of the city center. These are complicated organisms, actually consisting of two intricately associated partners, an alga and a fungus. In this cooperative relationship, called *symbiosis,* the algal component conducts the photosynthesis that feeds both partners and the fungus provides a tough structure in which the alga can safely dwell. Between them, they combine to form a very drought-resistant duo that can take a number of different shapes and sizes, dependent on the species. Most city lichens are crusts or leaflike scales on the surfaces of rock and brick faces. They are often most common in graveyards, where they coat the gravestones. Although lichens are highly resistant to desiccation, they are sensitive to air pollution, and increasing air pollution has resulted in the loss of many lichens from cities over the last 100 years. It is particularly the sulfur dioxide in the atmosphere produced by burning fossil fuels that has a harmful effect on the lichens. The fungal component is sensitive to sulfur and the alga is damaged by the acidity of the sulfuric acid caused by the sulfur dioxide dissolving in rainwater. Some lichens, however, are resistant to pollutant chemicals, the main one being *Lecanora conizaeoides,* which forms a grayish coating especially on trees in city parks. A rare species in Victorian times, which was outcompeted by other more robust lichens, it has become by far the most common lichen of cities over the last century. As atmospheric levels of sulfur fall, we are beginning to see a return of lichens to many of our cities in recent years.

Although bare soil may be scarce in the city, cracks between the segments of pavement on sidewalks do allow some plants to take root. The dandelion (*Taraxacum officinale*), for example, has many features that permit it to thrive in such situations. It disperses effectively by means of airborne seeds, each equipped with a parachute that reduces the rate at which it falls from the air and, therefore, gives it a better chance of being carried long distances. It germinates in any crevice where it may become lodged and then produces a deep taproot that penetrates through rubble until it reaches a source of water. Its leaves form a rosette that is well adapted to the hardships of trampling, and it may manage to flower and produce seeds under even the most adverse circumstances. As a last resort, if the flower head is broken, the seeds often manage to mature without the help of the rest of the plant. Meanwhile, the perennial root system is very difficult to remove. It fragments easily, and even a very small fragment that remains beneath the ground can regenerate into a new plant.

The butterfly bush (*Buddleia davidii*) is not quite as effective as the dandelion in colonizing sidewalks, but it can achieve an even more remarkable feat by invading vertical walls. The seeds are tiny and are easily dispersed, like dust, through the air. They land in all kinds of unlikely places, including the cracks and crevices in old walls, and here they may manage to germinate and establish themselves. They need quite moist conditions for their initial growth, so they are often found in sites where water drains from defective drainpipes and gutters around old roofs. Once established, the seed grows into a robust shrub that can survive for many years. A plant of similar habitats in the cities of southern Europe is the fig (*Ficus carica*). The fruits of this plant are consumed by birds, and the seeds pass though the gut and are deposited on walls when the bird releases its droppings. So the plant is conveyed very effectively to precisely the location where it best survives. Like the butterfly bush, figs germinate in the cracks in walls and grow into branching bushes, penetrating between the brickwork with its increasingly tenacious roots and doing much damage to the structure of the walls.

Dandelions are native to America, just as figs are native to the Mediterranean region of Europe, so these are local species that have adapted to the new opportunities offered by the cities. The butterfly bush, on the other hand, came originally from China and has been carried around and planted in gardens by people, eventually taking off on its own to spread as a weed into neglected parts of our cities. As these examples demonstrate, our city wildlife consists of a mixture of native species that have taken up the challenge of the city and imports from other parts of the world.

Animals in the city

The bird life of cities effectively illustrates the city's eclectic mix of species. The blue jays (*Cyanocitta cristata*) of Central Park in New York City and the scrub jays (*Aphelocoma californica*) of the Los Angeles suburbs are local woodland and scrubland species, respectively, that have found conditions very tolerable in the city. Some native birds, like the mourning dove (*Zenaida macroura*) and the Brewer's blackbird (*Euphagus cyanocephalus*), have become extremely common in cities. The Brewer's blackbird, in fact, has exploited both agricultural and urban habitats, forming large flocks over arable land, where it feeds mainly on soil insects, and also frequenting the shopping malls of many western cities, where it begs food from the human clientele of restaurants and bars. Domestic pigeons have been carried around the world by humans. We originally domesticated the rock dove (*Columba livia*) that inhabits the coastal cliffs of Europe as a source of food. The medieval dovecotes (a kind of birdhouse) that were found in every town provided a source of the feral (semi-wild) pigeons, descended from the rock dove, that now infest most of our cities. Pigeons are a nuisance in their roosting habits; they leave droppings over city buildings; and they can also carry disease. But their rapid breeding, omnivorous

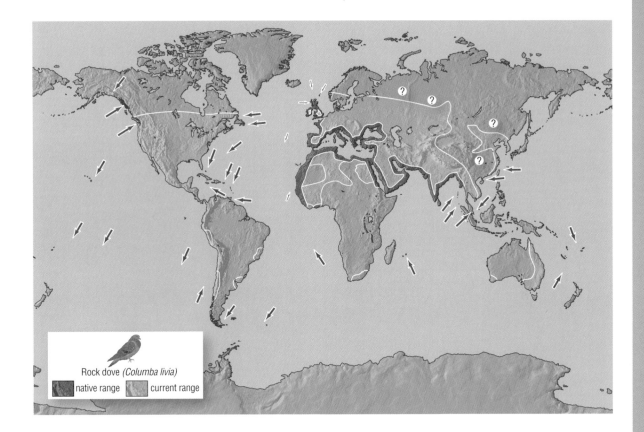

Rock dove *(Columba livia)*

native range   current range

diet, and adaptable nature have served them well, as pigeons occupy the new "cliffs" that we have provided in our concrete canyons. As a result of its association with humans, the rock dove has greatly extended its global distribution.

In order to exploit the city environment that humans have created, animals need to be able to develop new behavior patterns. Brewer's blackbirds can be found in wild scrublands, where they are relatively shy and avoid human contact. But in parking lots and urban areas, they have adopted a very different pattern of behavior, showing little fear of people and even becoming demanding if they perceive that there is food available. Squirrels have developed similar techniques. While they may fear humans as predators in wilderness locations, they become confident and even aggressive in urban parks and gardens. Undoubtedly, the urban animal trains its young in these very successful behavioral adaptations.

The original distribution pattern of the rock dove (Columba livia), *the common pigeon of our cities, in the Mediterranean and coastal regions of Europe and Africa, compared with its present distribution around the world. This coastal, cliff-inhabiting species has adopted human cities, towns, and villages as its new habitat.*

Some animals avoid the stress of human contact by conducting their activities at night. The raccoon (*Procyon lotor*), for example, is a widespread inhabitant of suburban habitats that combines its curiosity with a wide adaptability to habitats and lifestyles (see the sidebar). Raccoons are generally not a serious pest in towns, even though their destructive habits and their transport of disease can make them a source of danger. Woodchucks, also known as groundhogs (*Marmota monax*), dig tunnels under the ground in suburban gardens as well as on farms and in meadows. Their tunneling may make them unwelcome when they use lawns as their habitat, but in turning the soil, they are actually performing a valuable ecological task. It has been estimated that the woodchucks of New York State turn over 1.6 million tons of soil each year.

Some other mammals present an even greater problem, such as bears and mountain lions. The black bear (*Ursus amer-*

Raccoons: urban bandits

Few mammals have adapted to urban life as well as the raccoon. Raccoons sleep through the day, often sheltered in a tree, then roam at nightfall to scavenge in trash cans and anywhere else they can break and enter. They are omnivorous, enjoying french fries and doughnuts, but also having a taste for fish from garden ponds. Their hands are almost as dexterous as those of humans and this gives them the ability to manipulate doors and windows, making them excellent burglars. Like so many other animals that have adopted human habitats, they are able to expand their populations rapidly. A female is able to breed in its first year of life, and the litter size may be as high as six, but a raccoon in the wild rarely survives beyond 10 years. They live at quite high densities in North American cities, reaching about 160 per square mile in Toronto. Their masklike facial pattern gives them a roguish appearance, but their cute appearance is deceptive because they bring diseases that can spread to humans, including a potentially fatal roundworm parasite. The parasite lives in the intestine of the raccoon and does little damage to its host, but when the eggs are shed in feces they enter the soil and can be ingested by people, especially children. Infection of humans can lead to loss of sight, brain damage, or even death. So these attractive animals that share our cities can be a threat and need to be controlled.

icana) in North America is a mammal that has seen its own forest habitat decline as human land use has become more extensive. It has responded by changing its patterns of behavior to compensate for this loss and seeking out the easy pickings offered by the careless waste-disposal habits of humans. Like raccoons, bears that adopt the scavenging lifestyle can be extremely destructive, but their great strength can result in major damage and even danger to humans at times. Sometimes bears can be led into this way of life as a result of human carelessness with their waste food or even deliberate training of bears to take food for the sake of casual amusement. When bears become accustomed to this way of life, they may have to be physically removed or even destroyed due to the threat they then pose to humans. The mountain lion, or cougar (*Felis concolor*), is also becoming an increasing problem in certain cities, such as the suburbs of San Diego, California. The scrub habitat of this big predator has been eroded by housing and agricultural development, and the animals are having to turn to alternative habitats and food sources. In suburban areas domestic pets, such as dogs and cats, are easy prey. These examples show how animals under pressure as a result of habitat loss are forced to change their way of life and join us in the city, even though they may not be welcome there.

Many animals, however, are welcome among us, and many more go unnoticed. The warm air of the city in summer can be rich in insect life, and insects in turn attract such insectivores as the swifts and swallows that constantly sweep the skies to harvest them on the wing. At night they are replaced by bats and nighthawks, which often use the streetlights we helpfully provide as a means of attracting night-flying insects, such as moths. The chimney swift (*Chaetura pelagica*), as its name implies, uses buildings for its nesting sites, producing gluelike saliva to construct nests that must stick tightly to vertical walls. These birds have taken our buildings as a convenient alternative to natural cliff faces and adapted their way of life accordingly. Cliff swallows (*Petrochelidon pyrrhonota*), on the other hand, prefer the under surface of bridges under highways and railroad lines,

The white stork (Ciconia ciconia) *often uses urban rooftops or even power lines for its nesting sites in eastern Europe. Most people welcome these birds and regard their presence as a good luck omen.* (Courtesy of Wil Meinderts/ Foto Natura/ Minden Pictures)

where they construct nests, which resemble jugs with narrow, tubular necks, often in large colonies.

Human waste, especially when dumped in heaps or landfill sites, provides a rich resource for the scavengers that have joined us in cities. Many such dumps become inhabited by large flocks of gulls that are always ready to leave their normal habitat when easy pickings are available. In southern Africa, it is a stork, the marabou stork (*Leptopilos crumeniferus*), that has taken on the role of clearing up our spare waste. These huge, disreputable-looking birds circle around the waste heaps on stiff wings, and then sit with hunched shoulders as they await the arrival of new resources. The European white stork (*Ciconia ciconia*) is a more elegant bird, and its nest upon human habitations is regarded as an omen of good fortune.

The crow family has proved extremely adaptable to city life. Crows, jays, and magpies, all members of this family, are often associated with cities, the black crows themselves (genus *Corvus*) being the members that are most likely to be encountered in city centers. The long-legged American crow (*Corvus brachyrhynchos*) is found in virtually all U.S. cities. In Europe it is the carrion crow (*Corvus corone*) that occupies this role in city life, while in India it is the house crow (*Corvus splendens*). In Africa south of the Sahara, the black-and-white pied crow (*Corvus alba*) lives alongside people in the villages and towns. In the remote villages of Iran, another type of crow, the red-billed chough (*Pyrrhocorax pyrrhocorax*), forms flocks that gather around areas of human occupation. Evidently a certain affinity exists between crows and people. Crows are intelligent birds that are very adaptable in their habits. They become cautious when persecuted but lose this shyness when left in peace. They are omnivorous, though they do favor meat when it is available, so they can flourish on the waste products of human occupation. Wherever human have settled, the local crow species seems to have benefited from becoming our close associate.

Although most crows are resident local birds, some other members of the bird life of cities have come from far away. Take the house sparrow, or English sparrow (*Passer domestic-*

A male house sparrow (Passer domesticus). This sociable bird was introduced into North America from Europe and has become a common city resident. (Courtesy of Wouter van Caspel)

urs), for example. This is not a true New World sparrow, but is closer to the buntings and weaver finches in its origin. It is native to Europe and Asia and is likely to have originated in dry grassland habitats with scattered trees. It still occupies such locations in the Middle East, where it often nests in communal groups in trees, constructing domed nests with entrances in one side that hang in woven hammocks from tree branches. When humans began constructing shacks and houses to protect themselves from the elements, they provided an ideal habitat for sparrow nesting, under overhangs, within thatch, and between shingles. Our ancestors also provided an ideal source of food as they cultivated grain and inevitably left some in the soil during harvest. So the house sparrow became attached to human habitations and subsequently became one of the most successful and common birds of the Old World. It was not found in America, but the Old World human colonists decided to introduce it. Whether this was out of nostalgia for the Old Country or because they thought it might solve some insect pest problems is unclear. (Especially when feeding its young, the house sparrow does eat insects, including the dropworm, larva of the snow-white linden moth, which is a pest in New England.) Perhaps both motives played a part. The bird was first brought to the United States in 1850, when just eight pairs were introduced to Brooklyn, New York. By all accounts, the introduction was not successful and the birds died out. Undeterred, the sparrow enthusiasts brought over another 100 birds in 1852 and released them in the Greenwood Cemetery in Brooklyn. This proved successful, as did other East Coast introductions at Portland, Maine, in 1854, and in Boston, New York, Philadelphia, and Quebec City in subsequent years. Their spread was not rapid (25 miles in five years, 50 miles in 10 years, and 100 miles in 15 years), but additional introductions and transplants of populations across the continent ensured its success in colonizing North America. The house sparrow is now well established and common from northern Ontario to southern Mexico. The same story has been enacted through much of the temperate world.

The European starling (*Sturnus vulgaris*), as can be seen from the map, has a similar history. Again, it has its origins in

Europe and western Asia, being originally a bird of open grasslands and steppes, breeding in holes in trees or in rock crevices on cliffs. In the case of the starling, the agricultural development that most suited it was the spread of grazing animals. Constant grazing, especially by sheep, reduced woodland habitats to short-turf grasslands where the starling proved very successful. It forages in flocks over short grassland, probing the soil with an open beak that is able to detect the presence of invertebrate animals, particularly larvae of crane flies. After a day's work, these flocks roost communally, either in trees or, preferably, on cliff faces. The creation of cities, with their high concrete buildings with convenient

The spread of the European starling (Sturnus vulgaris) through North and Central America following its introduction to New York in the 19th century. Originally a bird of cliffs and grasslands, it has found suitable alternative habitats in cities and on farms.

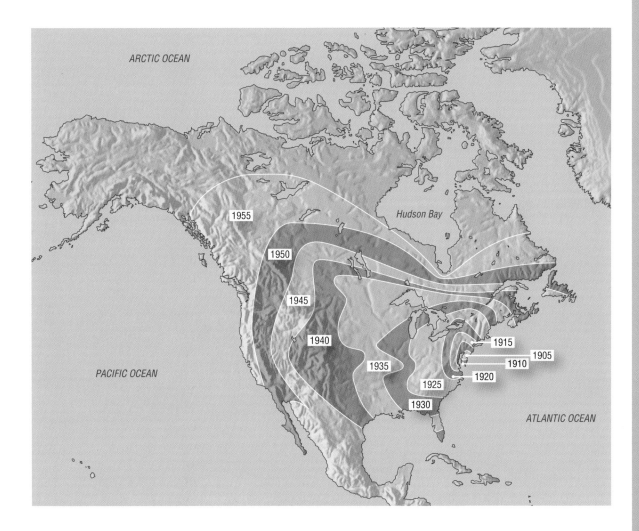

window ledges for roosting, gave starlings exactly what they needed for the expansion of their populations. Combining tall buildings with urban grasslands in lawns, recreation areas, and parks, cities supplied the starling with excellent sources of food, so its success was assured. Like the house sparrow, but for different reasons, cities proved ideal habitats for the starling.

Colonists of the New World found it lacking starlings. Grackles were present, but evidently these were not an adequate substitute for homesick Europeans, so starlings were introduced into America in 1890, when 60 birds were released in New York City's Central Park. Unlike that of the house sparrow, its spread through North America was largely unassisted by people, but it was equally successful, as can be seen from the map. The starling now occupies a range in North America similar to that of the house sparrow, and it has been transported to other parts of the world, especially southern Africa, Australia, and New Zealand, where it has become an important component of city wildlife.

Urban pests

Since we do not generally grow food crops in our cities, we do not need to worry about pests that might attack them. But we do store food in warehouses, shops, and homes, so animal pests do exist in the city. Pests may also damage the materials of our buildings, consume the plants we keep in our gardens, or even carry disease, so the war against pests is just as active in cities as in rural areas.

Rats and mice probably spring to mind when we think of urban animal pests, and rightly so. The common, or brown, rat (*Rattus norvegicus*) and the house mouse (*Mus musculus*) are among the most successful animals of cities. The rat is able to live away from human dwellings, in riverbanks and marshes, but is also very successful in association with humans, both in rural and in urban settings. The house mouse, on the other hand, has become almost totally dependent on people and is rarely found away from our farms and cities. The brown rat, also known as the Norway rat, is an Old World species. It probably originated in southern Asia and quickly became an associate of humans when agriculture resulted in a need for seed storage, an ideal source of food for the rat. Like the crows, it has a very wide range of diet, from meat to cereals, preferring food items that are rich in protein or in starch. Since it burrows beneath the ground, the rat is capable of coping with a wide range of climates, escaping underground from excessive heat or frost, but it is happiest within the temperate zone. It can live in drains and sewers or on board ships, which have provided it with an ideal means of transport with its human host. The brown rat is also a prolific breeder. Its gestation period (the time for which a female carries her young) is only three to four weeks, and the litter size can be as high as 12. Given that a female rat is able to bear up to five litters a year, it is clear that the rate of increase in population under good conditions is potentially very high. Like crows, rats are very intelligent creatures; inquisitive and daring, they are full of initiative when it comes to taking advantage of new situations. For this reason, like crows, they can actually become very good pets.

The problem with rats is that they are not content with living alongside us in the way that crows do. They steal our stored foods, and this cannot be tolerated. Moreover, they do not simply steal food, they also damage the produce that they leave behind. By breaking open storage containers, rats cause much unused food to be lost, and they also deposit fecal material and hair that damages the quality of the remaining food, infecting it with salmonella (a cause of food poisoning) and other microbes. Rats also carry a disease organism called leptospirosis. This spiral-shaped parasite is passed in the urine of the rat and can infect humans, where it causes headaches, rash, vomiting, liver damage, and sometimes meningitis or heart disease. It is not surprising that the rat is not a popular organism. Its arrival in North America in the late 18th century was inevitable, given the ability of the animal to travel with humans, but it was an unfortunate event for the New World.

The black rat (*Rattus rattus*) is very similar to the brown rat, but it is even more confined to city habitats, especially seaports, and is more successful in the Tropics. The black rat spread before the brown rat, and it was the dominant rat in

Europe from prehistoric times through the 16th century, when it began to be displaced by the brown rat. Its major claim to fame (or infamy) is that it is host to fleas that carry plague to human beings. The bubonic plague kills the rat too. When the rat dies, the fleas abandon the corpse and may then move to nearby humans as an alternative host, carrying the disease organism with them. We know that plague epidemics were regular events in ancient Rome. During these episodes, records show, 5,000 people died each day from the disease. Its spread through the Roman Empire killed as many as 100 million people. The most devastating pandemic of bubonic plague, the Black Death, however, took place in Europe and Asia in the 1330s and 1340s. Its impact was greatest in the cities, where crowded, unhygienic conditions and thriving black rat populations allowed it to spread quickly. In many cities half of the population died of the plague. Outbreaks continued into the 17th century, including the Great Plague of London in 1665, but by the end of that century the disease began to die out. There are many ideas about why this was so. The brown rat was replacing the black rat in Europe and seaports were becoming stricter about quarantine laws for ships from the east, and black rats became less common as stowaways. The rat may have been developing a degree of immunity to the disease, or the disease organism itself may have become less virulent. Also, the climate was becoming increasingly cold, and perhaps the black rat was less able to succeed in these conditions. Whatever the cause, bubonic plague has become a less serious threat to our species in recent times, but our dislike of the rat has persisted.

Cities and disease

We now know that many diseases are caused by microscopic organisms that occupy the human body and are passed from one person to another. It is easy to understand, therefore, that in places where large groups of people gather, such as cities, the spread of disease will always be a problem. But we have only come to appreciate the causes of disease during the last 150 years or so, and prior to that physicians were hard pressed to account for the way in which disease spread.

A classic disease of settled human communities is typhoid fever, which is spread by fecal material infecting drinking water supplies. This is unlikely in rural communities or among nomadic pastoralists, because the two activities (eating and drinking versus defecating) can be well separated. But in cities, the privy and the well were often placed close together, and the possibility of percolation of infectious organisms through the soil was not appreciated. General lack of hygiene, unwashed hands, flies transporting microbes from dung heap to food, and poor sanitation all provide ideal conditions for the spread of typhoid fever. Early physicians recognized that this sickness, which often kills 10 to 20 percent of sufferers in the absence of medication, was associated with poverty and dirty conditions, but it was not until 1839 that the possibility of its being a contagious disease, rather than a poison from evil smells, was seriously considered. When Prince Albert, the husband of Queen Victoria of the United Kingdom, died of typhoid in 1858, attention was focused on the disease. But it was not until 1870 that a German scientist, Robert Koch (1843–1910), discovered the organism in the body of a victim and demonstrated that this bacterium caused it. One of the problems with typhoid is that some people act as carriers without showing the symptoms of the disease, and they can be quite dangerous to the general public. One famous case involved Mary Mallon (1870?–1938), an Irish immigrant to New York from 1904, who worked in 1906 as a cook and whose succession of employers contracted typhoid. Coming to be known as Typhoid Mary, she was traced and jailed because she refused to accept the danger she represented. On release, Mallon disappeared, only to turn up as a cook in a hospital, so she was jailed again in 1914, where she remained until her death in 1938.

It is the close contact that exists between people in cities that provides the right conditions for diseases like typhoid to flourish. Another city-spread disease, cholera, is also caused by a bacterium. It survives well outside the human body, so infected clothing, water sources, or any other contaminated material assists the dissemination of the disease. The history of cholera is one of successive waves of global expansion, often originating in the Indian subcontinent and radiating through the world. It first came to world notice in 1817, when it spread along the major trade routes. Around 30 million people are likely to have died from this disease in the second half of the 19th century. In cities, cholera epidemics were most likely caused by the contamination of water supplies, but it took a long while to prove this. Working in London, England, in 1854, a young physician named John Snow (1813–58) conducted a careful study of the occurrence of cholera in part of the city and found that all those infected in this area were dependent on a single water source, which was the fount of the disease. The city to exploit these findings most rapidly was New York, which provided a clean water supply for cholera control as soon as the disease was detected. In this way, the city authorities quickly controlled an outbreak in 1866.

Like bacterial diseases, parasites such as tapeworms and roundworms are transmitted through fecal contamination, and these have also become less common in the developed world as a result of better standards of hygiene. But many parasitic diseases remain a serious problem in developing nations. Schistosomiasis, or bilharzia, is a tropical disease found mainly in Africa, eastern South America, and Southeast Asia. It is caused by a parasitic worm that spends part of its life cycle in an aquatic snail. The snail sheds larvae into the water and, if they encounter bare human skin, they penetrate it and enter the human bloodstream. They settle in the blood vessels of the intestine or the bladder and produce eggs, which are released into the feces or the urine. If these contaminate water supplies, then they are taken up by snails and the cycle continues. It is believed that more than 200 million people are currently infected with the disease worldwide, and the main control is to maintain uncontaminated water supplies. In many cities, suburbs, and rural communities, this is difficult, and work is proceeding on drugs to control the parasite in the human body and pesticides to destroy the snail in the aquatic habitats.

Despite recent success in controlling many serious diseases of cities, the close proximity of people will always present problems in disease spread. Tuberculosis, for example, is easily spread in crowded places, especially when living conditions are poor. It is also a disease that is rapidly developing resistance to the drugs that controlled it during the last century, and it may well prove a new challenge to city medicine in the 21st century. Influenza is still a common city disease, spread through the aerial transmission of a virus in crowded rooms, commuter trains, and offices. Although unpleasant, it is rarely fatal among young healthy people, but it can be a severe threat to older people and to those weakened by poor diet or living conditions. The development of vaccines as a preventative has helped to avoid loss of life as a result of influenza, but the virus evolves rapidly and produces new strains each year, so vaccines need to be constantly updated to keep abreast of the evolution of the disease. The possibility of new virulent strains, such as the Chinese "bird flu," evolving remains high, and rapid global spread is now simple, given the speed and ease of transport in modern times.

Urban biodiversity

Clearly there is no shortage of wild plants, animals, and microbes in the city, some welcome and many not so welcome, as in the case of disease microbes and the animals that carry them. Many organisms have accompanied us as we have settled into large communities with complex mosaic structures, all of them adapting to the new conditions and taking advantage of the new opportunities. Some of these organisms are harmful and we take elaborate, and often expensive, measures to eliminate them. Others are relatively neutral as far as our health and welfare are concerned. They join us in the habitat we have created but they neither harm nor benefit us greatly, apart from the pleasure we may gain by their very presence.

Many of the animals and plants that accompany us in our cities owe their presence to the transport we have provided. As a species, we are almost unique in the animal kingdom in taking pleasure in the presence of other species of plants and animals around us, and for this reason we have created parks and gardens for our aesthetic enjoyment rather than simply for food supply. We have carried plants and animals from one part of the world to another usually to enhance our immediate biodiversity and perhaps to remind us of other places we have visited or lived. Sometimes the plants and animals we have introduced to our cities have been more successful than we had anticipated and have become abundant, even assuming pest status, but this is not invariably the case.

As is most ecosystems, biodiversity in cities is closely linked to habitat diversity. The cities that contain the greatest range of plant and animal species are those with a large range of urban habitats, including city parks with lakes and wetland areas, rivers that have not been canalized or diverted into underground tunnels, diverse gardens and open grassland areas, and an abundance of trees. We can create biodiversity around us and thus enhance the quality of our lives. The creation and conservation of biodiversity in cities and farmland will be the subject of chapter 6.

Conclusions

Biodiversity means the complete range of living species found in an area, together with the amount of genetic variation within each species. In both farms and cities we have modified the natural biodiversity of the areas we have settled. We have selected a limited number of animals and plants that we find useful or decorative and have permitted them to share our living space. Many of our domestic animals and plants were brought into captivity around 10,000 years ago, so there remain many opportunities to expand the range of organisms that serve us.

Although we have greatly altered the habitats present in the areas we have settled, our farms and cities still maintain a wide range of creatures. We tend to produce a very fragmented and varied environment with patches of different habitats present. Farms may have open fields, pastures, hedges, ponds, and woodlands. Cities may have urban parks, lakes, grasslands, and gardens. All of these serve to enhance biodiversity and may create a rich collection of plants and animals. High human density does not necessarily mean low biodiversity; quite the reverse is true.

Some of the organisms that share our farms and cities are native to the area and have adopted the new habitats we have created. Plants that once grew in naturally disturbed areas, such as riverbanks, steep hill slopes, and areas damaged by wind or fire, have now become the weeds of our fields and gardens. They are generally short-lived and have a high seed production and dispersal ability. Animals of woodlands and grasslands, including squirrels, raccoons, crows, jays, and robins, have adapted to the new conditions and the new sources of food that our farms and cities have provided. But we have also carried some species around the world with us, either deliberately or by accident. Many of the birds we take for granted in our gardens, for example, including starlings and house sparrows, are there because humans have transported them around the world. Human beings have changed the whole pattern of global biogeography.

Some species have become pests. Rats and rabbits consume our food or that of our domesticated animals. Purple loosestrife has spread over our riverbanks and excluded some of our native plants. In trying to combat these pests, we have invented chemical poisons that have had wide-ranging impacts on natural ecosystems and have sometimes succeeded in creating more devastation than the pests themselves. Among the most serious pest organisms are the disease-causing microbes that infest our cities and find it easy to spread among the crowded populations of their hosts. Cities have long proved to be disease centers, and the speed and efficiency of human transport systems is providing our parasites and pathogens with a rapid and easy means of dispersal.

Like any other ecosystem, farms and cities have their own diverse assemblage of organisms. People face the dilemma of eliminating those species that are regarded as pests and at the same time enhancing the biodiversity of the animals and plants we have gathered around us.

CHAPTER 5

THE HISTORY AND PREHISTORY OF FARMS AND CITIES

Farmland and cities are so much a part of our modern environment that we tend to take them for granted. It is difficult to imagine that Manhattan was once a forest, or that Las Vegas was once part of the open desert, or that the Grain Belt was once a prairie with roaming herds of bison. Great changes have occurred over the last few hundred years. Many of the features of farms and cities that have been considered so far, such as why they developed where they did, why cities have distinct zones, how the two ecosystems interact with each other, and where the animals and plants that share our environment came from, all relate to history. Hence an appreciation of the history of farms and cities can help us understand their present structure and activities.

The end of the Ice Age

Fifteen thousand years ago, not very long when one considers the 4.5 billion years that the Earth has existed, the world was a very different place. The Ice Age was coming to an end, but vast sheets of ice still covered the northern areas of North America, Europe, and parts of Asia, as well as the high mountain regions farther south. Sea levels were much lower, perhaps by as much as 330 feet (100 m), so areas that are now part of the seabed were then dry land, including the region that links eastern Russia with what is now Alaska. Evidence from fossil insects suggests that the climate rapidly became warmer; in a matter of decades in some places, the average temperature rose by several degrees.

In this unstable climate, plants and animals were thrown into confusion. Most animals are mobile, and many of them would have been able to adjust to the change very quickly, moving poleward and changing their patterns of distribution as conditions became warmer. Flying animals, including many insects, birds, and bats, would have been the most responsive, soon colonizing new regions, while animals restricted to ground movements would have followed in their wake. Plants are generally less mobile. They have to depend on the spread of fruits and seeds to occupy new areas, and then they must wait until the new individual reaches maturity before it can produce new fruits and make the next step forward. Many trees are particularly slow in responding to climate change, such as the oak, which takes a long time to mature and has to depend on animals, such as jays, pigeons, and squirrels, to disperse its heavy acorns. Even so, a look at the pace at which oak trees extended their range northward after the last Ice Age, reveals the surprising expansion rate of about 1,000 feet (300 m) per year. The forests were marching northward through the temperate zone as the ice sheets melted.

Among the many species on the move was *Homo sapiens,* the sole member of the genus *Homo* to emerge successfully from the Ice Age. Our close relative, Neanderthal man, had become extinct during this cold period. Our ancestors were hunters, feeding upon the large herbivores that abounded at that time, including mammoths, giant elk, and giant sloth, as well as animals that are more familiar today, such as caribou and the common elk. We were not the only predators feeding upon these prey animals; bears (including giant cave bears), wolves, and large cats hunted the same game. As our competitors in the hunt, and sometimes also our predators, these animals were unwelcome neighbors and humans eliminated them whenever the opportunity offered itself.

The first domesticates

Among the numerous predators that emerged with us from the Ice Age was one animal whose pattern of behavior made it quite appealing to humans, the wolf (*Canis lupus*). Wolves are pack animals; they are accustomed to strict discipline within the pack, hunting according to team rules, and conducting activities communally. It is likely that they associated loosely with humans on their hunts, keeping their distance but being prepared to take advantage of any leftovers they could steal. It is very difficult to discover just how hunting techniques developed among the Stone Age peoples of these times, but primitive art on the walls of caves shows human hunters driving game animals over cliffs and into traps. It is possible that humans developed these hunting techniques by watching the wolves and perhaps even cooperating in driving prey animals into places where they were cornered and easily slaughtered. Given such coexistence between humans and wolves, it would have been only a small step for humans to capture young wolves and train them to obey new human pack masters in the hunt. This association seems to have served the wolf species well; in the world today there are certainly far more dogs (the domesticated wolf) than there are wild wolves.

Just how far back in prehistory do we have to go to locate this first domestication? It is quite difficult to be sure. There are records of human and wolf bones in association with one another as long ago as 400,000 years, but this could be chance or even a case of humans eating wolves. Careful comparison of the genetics of modern dogs and wolves has given clues about when domestication first took place, and the current estimate is 100,000 years ago. This is long before the end of the last Ice Age; indeed, it is during the warm period that preceded the last Ice Age. So the idea of domestication had evidently entered the heads of humans in the early stages of our history as a species.

While hunting cultures were still slaying mammoths in the north of Asia, other human populations occupied the warmer climates around the eastern end of the Mediterranean Sea. This is where many of the European and Asian oak species that were now headed north had survived during the height of the cold period, and an open oak woodland persisted around 12,000 years ago, in which people hunted and gathered the fruits of the forest. From the archaeological remains of these people we can deduce much about their way of life. They constructed weapons from small flakes of stone (especially obsidian, a dark glasslike material), which they embedded into bone or wooden shafts to make spears, arrows, and harpoons. With these weapons they hunted game, ranging from deer to fish.

There are few decorative or luxury objects associated with the people of this period, despite the fact that preceding and later cultures spent time developing their artistic talents. Some rock shelters in the south of Spain have engraved walls showing people engaged in dancing, which indicates that they had some leisure time, but most of their lives were probably taken up with hunting and food gathering.

By 11,000 years ago, however, some new objects began to appear in the archaeological record of the eastern Mediterranean lands. Some of these were crude stone basins, called *querns*, together with other stones evidently used for grinding food materials within the querns. Also present were new types of implements, including what appeared to be the curved blades of sickles, used for harvesting grasses. Archaeologists can only guess at what these imply, but the simplest explanation is that the people were becoming more sophisticated in their gathering techniques, cutting the fruiting heads from grasses that grew in the forest clearings and grinding the seeds in their querns to produce a kind of flour. Weapons for hunting and fishing were still present, so some of their food must still have come from these sources. Also of significance is the first appearance of decorative objects, beads, rings and necklaces, which suggests that these people had an artistic tendency and, even more important, the time to spend on leisure and the construction of luxury items. Burials took place beneath the floor of huts, which indicates a degree of religious activity and perhaps a belief in the survival of the spirits of their ancestors.

It is difficult to discern exactly when gathering activities became farming activities. One indication is the storage of grain from one year to the next for planting, but in the archaeological record this cannot easily be distinguished from storage for later consumption by people. There is evidence that pits were dug in the ground for grain storage, and the fossil remains of grass seeds show that grain was indeed kept within them. We must assume, however, that the people of that time were just as intelligent as our modern race, for their skulls demonstrate that the volume of their brains was as great as our own. They lived close to nature and were dependent upon the production of the native vegetation and the animals that fed upon it. They must, therefore, soon have come to understand that clearing woodland trees that shaded the grasses would lead to greater production of grain. Disturbing the soils in which the grasses grew could lead to better seed germination and the spread of grassland. It is then a short step to the point where people preserved seed through the unfavorable period of the year (probably the hot, dry summer in those dry regions of the Middle East) and then sowed it when the rains arrived in the fall. This was the first step in plant domestication. It has been described as the agricultural revolution, but this term is perhaps unduly dramatic for what was a gradual development of an idea. It is certainly true, however, that it was an idea that changed the course of human history.

Why did grasses become the first cultivated plants in this Middle Eastern area? Perhaps the most important reason is that the annual grasses of the region put most of their energy into the production of seeds so that they could persist in this form through the hot, dry summers. These grasses were intolerant of shade and were efficient colonists of dry, open clearings, flowering and fruiting in the warm, moist spring and early summer, then dying off as the heat became intense. At this stage the fruiting heads with their rich crop of seeds could easily be harvested by hand with stone sickles, and people ground the starch-rich seeds in querns to provide a nutritious food source. The most important grasses were wild varieties of wheat, which grew abundantly in that area. In their lifestyles these wild wheat varieties resembled weeds in that they were well adapted to living in very unstable soils and succeeded because of their high level of seed production (see "Weeds," pages 111–119). Like the wolf, however, these plants benefited greatly by association with human populations, for their survival from year to year was assured and the farmers spent time and effort in creating the right conditions for their growth. Agriculture was born.

Pastoral farmers

At this time, around 11,000 to 9,000 years ago, many different tribes and peoples were living throughout the Middle

East. Some inhabited the mountain regions of what is now Turkey and Iran, and among them were the people who domesticated the sheep (genus *Ovis*). Wild sheep still wander around the remote hills of the Iranian deserts. They are large, long-eared, and long-legged animals that are swift and agile. Wild sheep had long been a major prey animal of the ancient hill people, but a great deal of effort had to be expended in hunting and killing them, so there was much to be gained by capturing young animals and raising them to maturity. This strategy provided meat with less effort expended. Once again, it is a small step from keeping herds of captive animals to the controlled breeding and maintenance of flocks from which some animals can be regularly harvested for food. The change from general hunting to the keeping of flocks can be detected in the archaeological record by checking bone assemblages associated with campsites. When domestication occurs, the diversity of animal species represented in the bones declines. Instead of relying on many different kinds of prey, it is usually just one species, the sheep, that predominates. Human diet, therefore, became less diverse but more dependable. As in the case of other domesticated plants and animals, the sheep benefited, being assured of good grazing and protection from other predators, so its numbers increased. Pastoral farmers discovered that other products could be harvested from sheep in a sustainable fashion, namely wool and milk. Farmers selected certain characteristics in the wool of the domesticated sheep. The dark pigments of wild sheep were lost, the sheep no longer molted and lost their wool each year, and the wool became finer in texture. Maintaining a herd of sheep certainly took some of the stress and unpredictability out of life.

Following the domestication of sheep, and then goats (genus *Capra* and others), in the Middle East, cattle (especially genus *Bos*) and pigs (*Sus scrofa*) became the next focus of attention. Besides the presence of bones in archaeological settings, other evidence suggests that cattle were domesticated later than sheep and goats, perhaps around 8,000 years ago. Art from the walls of an ancient temple (about 2400 B.C.E.) in the city of Ur (in what is now Iraq) shows the activity of milking cattle, and the person thus occupied is sitting

The main centers where agriculture first developed, together with the regions from which various domesticated plants and animals originated

immediately behind the cow while manipulating its udder. Although this is a reasonable way to milk a goat or a sheep, it is not very advisable when dealing with cattle. If the animal is irritated, it is likely to kick out with its hind legs and this could be quite disastrous for the farmworker who is sitting right behind the tail. Milking from the side is the convention for cattle, but it appears that the early exponents of this art used the same system as they had devised for goats and sheep. No doubt they learned new techniques the hard way.

The domestication of animals and plants is best document-ed in the Middle East simply because archaeological remains are relatively abundant and much effort has been expended in

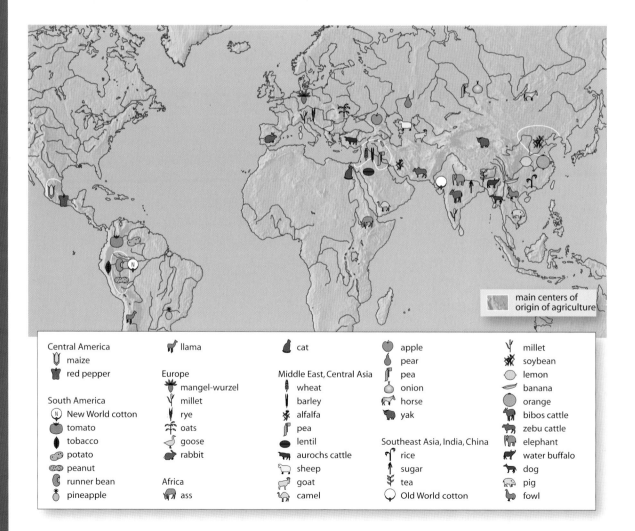

main centers of origin of agriculture

Central America		cat	apple	millet
U maize	llama		pear	soybean
red pepper	Europe	Middle East, Central Asia	pea	lemon
	mangel-wurzel	wheat	onion	banana
South America	millet	barley	horse	orange
New World cotton	rye	alfalfa	yak	bibos cattle
tomato	oats	pea		zebu cattle
tobacco	goose	lentil	Southeast Asia, India, China	elephant
potato	rabbit	aurochs cattle	rice	water buffalo
peanut		sheep	sugar	dog
runner bean	Africa	goat	tea	pig
pineapple	ass	camel	Old World cotton	fowl

studying the region over the last few centuries. But the idea arose independently in many different parts of the world. The Middle East gave us the four important domesticated animals already mentioned: sheep, goat, cow, and pig. Meanwhile, chickens (*Gallus gallus*) were being domesticated in Southeast Asia, and llamas (*Lama glama*), guinea pigs (*Cavia porcellus*), and alpacas (*Lama pacos*) in the Andes of South America. Later came the domestication of rabbits (*Oryctolagus cuniculus*) in Spain, camels (genus *Camelus*) in Arabia, elephants (*Elephas maximus*) in India, horses (*Equus caballus*) and donkeys (*Equus asinus*) in Asia, and cats (*Felis catus*) in Egypt. Many of these species were undoubtedly domesticated independently in several different places and using different varieties of wild animals. Cattle, for example, certainly had more than one center of origin, with a definite source of domestication in India as well as that of the Middle East.

Some animals were not strictly domesticated but were conserved and hunted by humans in a way that did not adversely affect their populations. In northern Europe, for example, the Lapp people of Scandinavia followed the wandering herds of reindeer (*Rangifer tarandus;* the same species as the North American caribou) and harvested from them a crop of meat and hides. Only later did they domesticate them fully and also use them as working animals, pulling sledges and the like. In North America, the Native Americans of the Great Plains harvested from the herds of bison (*Bison bison*) without causing any catastrophic overkill and extinction. Similarly, in central and western Europe, hunters concentrated their attention on the red deer (*Cervus elaphus;* the same species as the North American elk), and again the species did not seem to suffer as a result of this predation. Why was it that some of these large herbivorous animals were able to sustain the concentrated predatory attentions of people without suffering decline? The answer may be the manner of human predation, which differs from that of wild predators. Wolves and lions usually attack the very young animals or the very old and infirm. The result is that there are two periods in the life history of the population when death rates are at their greatest, shown by the steep declines in the accompanying figure. Ecologists would say that the young animals

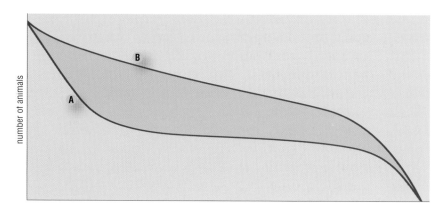

The age structure of an animal population when under natural and human predation. (A) Under natural predation, there is a high rate of mortality among the very young, which limits the number of animals surviving to breed in their middle years. (B) Under human predation, the young are often protected, leading to higher numbers of breeding animals and faster population growth.

and the old suffer the greatest rate of mortality. In between, the adult animals are at their fittest, so they usually survive quite well.

When humans prey upon a grazing herd in a conservation-minded way, they avoid the young and the breeding females and concentrate on older animals or males, which are often present in higher numbers than are strictly required for the maintenance of the herd. This reduces infant mortality and allows more animals to survive into the mature and breeding stages of the life cycle. In this way, a herd may actually increase in its size when subjected to human predation as compared with wild predation. Such animals as bison, reindeer, and elk undoubtedly thrived as humans conserved their stock and protected them from other predators, while still harvesting them for meat and hides. In this way, humans learned that sustainable harvesting of wild animals was a possibility.

Domestication and breeding

Managing the populations of plants and animals and harvesting some of their produce is only the first stage of the long process of domestication. The next stage is selection. Nature itself is a very efficient selector. Among the many seeds produced by a plant or the many young by an animal, there is a great deal of variation and only those that are best suited to their environment ("the fittest") survive. So, over the course of successive generations, an organism becomes better able to cope with the pressures of life that the species experiences. Human beings have applied the same approach when they select from among their domestic animals and plants for breeding, but the criteria used for selection do not always fit in with nature's normal requirements for "fitness." Take dogs, for example. It is difficult to believe that all the range of dog varieties found in the world today have resulted from the wolf, but that is what the genetic evidence tells us. Over the millennia, humans have selected for a whole range of characteristics, some of them quite sensible, such as speed, strength, or an acute sense of smell, which can be useful in a hunting dog. But some of the features we have favored are far from useful. The barrel chest of a bulldog can result in the development of respiratory problems, and the small size and delicacy of some "toy" dogs would certainly not be useful to them in the wild. But, whatever the criteria we have used for breeding, we have certainly been able to alter the appearance and the various qualities of our domesticated organisms.

As an example of the breeding process, consider wheat (genus *Triticum*), which, as we have already seen, was domesticated around 11,000 years ago in the Middle East. The very first type of wheat is called *einkorn* (scientific name *Triticum monococcum*), and it still exists as a wild plant in that part of the world. Some very sensitive genetic analyses have enabled scientists to locate the actual place where einkorn was first brought into domestication, in the Karacadag Mountains in the southeast of what is now Turkey. This wheat species proved very productive and was able to survive in many different types of soil and climate, so its use continued through Europe and Asia for several thousand years. Meanwhile, other varieties were being discovered and used. Einkorn is capable of interbreeding with other wild species of wheat, as shown in the figure, but generally such hybrids are infertile and thus are of no use to agriculturalists. Plants have an unusual mechanism of coping with infertility among hybrids, however: They double the number of chromosomes in their cells. Chromosomes carry all the genetic information of a cell. To produce reproductive cells (pollen and egg cells), chromosomes must form pairs and then split up. Hybrids are often incapable of doing this because they may have received a different number of chromosomes from each parent, meaning that when it is time for chromosomes to pair up, some are left without a partner. But if the chromosome number is doubled, then each chromosome is guaranteed to find a compatible partner during the reproductive process. So, a plant with doubled chromosome numbers is fertile once again despite being a hybrid.

As the illustration shows, two new types of wheat were formed in this way, and one of them, emmer wheat, proved to be more productive and to have bigger seeds than einkorn. So, a new type of wheat was born and its use spread through the agricultural world. This is still not the modern bread-making wheat that we use today, however. That species arose by yet another crossing with a wild wheat species that is found in modern Iran. Once again, there was a doubling of chromosomes and the result was the most productive of all the wheat types, the bread wheat. Productivity was the most important feature that was sought in the selection of early wheat species, but there was another characteristic that was almost as important. In order to be harvested efficiently, the wheat grains must be easily detached from the central stem. This quality has been bred into cultivated wheat. The process of selection continues, aiming for features such as salt tolerance, drought tolerance, and early germination. But today the use of laborious breeding programs can be avoided by using genetic manipulation. The possible repercussions of this technique, however, are still hotly debated.

In the New World the most important crop to emerge was corn, or maize (*Zea mays*). Some mystery surrounds the origin of maize, but it almost certainly came originally from Mexico. Unlike wheat, maize does not survive as a wild plant, so it is very difficult to be absolutely sure of its origin. There is a similar, and closely related, Mexican wild plant called *teosinte,* but it differs quite considerably in its flower structure, so its identity as the actual ancestor of maize has always been in doubt. Modern research, however, suggests that teosinte is indeed the ancestor. The archaeological record for corn, unlike that of wheat, shows no evidence of the wild plant prior to full domestication, so the change from teosinte to maize has gone unrecorded in the fossil history of the species. Perhaps some

T. searsil
(14)

T. speltoides
(14)

T. turgidum
(28)
(Emmer)

T. timopheevii
(28)

T. monococcum
(14)
(Einkorn)

T. tauschii
(14)

T. aestivum
(42)
(bread wheat)

The evolution of modern bread wheat (Triticum aestivum). *The numbers in parentheses are the numbers of chromosomes in a cell. Plants often evolve by doubling the number of chromosomes in the cell, a process called polyploidy. This process has been particularly important in the development of different varieties of wheat.*

remarkable mutation took place spontaneously in the ancestor of maize, and the new plant was born in an evolutionary leap. Certainly the archaeological record gives this impression, as the plant appears apparently out of nowhere.

In domestic animals the process of selective breeding was easier to control than in plants. Wheat and maize are pollinated by the wind, so selective breeding can only be achieved by the removal of the male parts from a plant and the artificial application of pollen from the selected partner. But in animals, male stud animals can be selected and used for the fertilization of individual females in a carefully controlled manner. This has led to a wide range of varieties in both cattle and sheep. In the case of cattle, for example, there is the question of whether the breed is to be used for milk or for beef production. For sheep, the quality of wool may be more important than the quality of the meat, depending on the main purpose of keeping the flocks. Disease resistance, climatic preferences, responses to parasites, and general strength of constitution, all these qualities require attention from the animal breeder. As in the case of plant crops, the role of genetic manipulation is likely to become more important as we produce designer animals for our different purposes.

When humans domesticated certain animals and plants, they took the place of nature in determining their future evolution. They imposed a new set of demands upon their domesticated organism, requiring animals to become docile and fat and obliging plants to put more energy into the production of fruit and seeds. In many cases this resulted in the domestic species becoming less able to cope on its own in nature and to become increasingly dependent on humans for its survival. By selective breeding we have reconstructed species to our own special requirements.

The spread of agriculture

Once the idea of agriculture had arisen in its various centers around the world, its success ensured its spread to new regions. The more reliable and profuse provision of food that resulted from agriculture led to population expansion, and surplus populations moved out from the points of origin literally to new pastures. The spread of agriculture has been traced in some detail in Europe and is shown in the figure. It was not a rapid spread; it took more than 4,000 years for agriculture to travel from the Middle East to the British Isles and

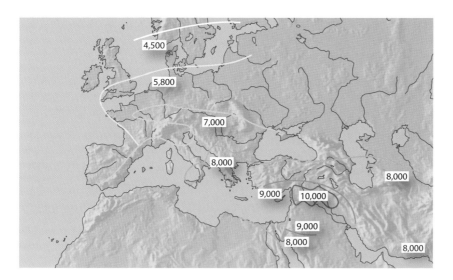

The spread of agriculture through Europe from its site of origin in the Fertile Crescent of Mesopotamia. The figures are derived from radiocarbon dating of agricultural remains and are given in the number of years before present.

more than 5,000 years to reach Scandinavia. This suggests that there was not a "gold rush" of people out to the distant parts of the continent with their flocks and sacks of grain, but that each part of the expansion was quite limited. Perhaps pioneers from a growing family would travel over the next ridge of hills with their domesticated animals and plants, clear some forest, and settle on the newly cleared land. The spread of agriculture in Europe actually took place more slowly than had the spread of forests at the end of the Ice Age.

In fact, the main brake on agricultural spread was probably the forest itself. The people of this period had no metal tools. All clearance had to be carried out using stone axes, together with the use of fire to consume the underbrush. Fire worked well as a clearing agent around the Mediterranean region, where summers are hot and dry and the forest burns easily. But farther north, where the climate is cooler and wetter, clearing forest by fire is a much more challenging task. Some archaeologists in Denmark attempted the backbreaking experiment of clearing an area of beech forest using just the tools of the Stone Age (borrowed from a local museum). It was hard work and slow, but it did prove possible. The larger trees were the most difficult, and these were best dealt with by cutting away a complete ring of bark around the trunk.

Just beneath the bark is the most important part of the trunk, for these are the living cells that keep dividing to produce new wood and bark and also the cells that carry food from the leaves down to the roots. Removing a complete ring of bark kills a tree. It still takes several years, however, for the dead tree to become sufficiently weakened to allow it to be felled with a stone ax or to be sufficiently flammable for removal by fire.

Despite these problems, agriculture moved slowly northward through Europe until, by around 4,500 years ago, the entire continent had been brought into agricultural development. Only the locations that had poor, shallow soils, were flooded, or were at high altitude with short growing seasons were left undisturbed by the plow. Even these sites were often subjected to the pressures of grazing animals, so that truly natural vegetation became very scarce and fragmented.

The process of agricultural spread has left clear marks in the archaeology of Europe. Records of forest clearance, with increasing grassland and open land, are also to be found in the sediments of lakes and bogs. In the successive layers of these wetlands, the pollen grains that rained down from the air in times past are preserved as fossils, and these record the declining tree pollen and increasing grass pollen as agricultural peoples arrived in an area and set to work. In the New World the spread of agriculture has been more difficult to trace because the Native American way of life involved only local forest clearance and then abandonment, so long-term impacts are much more difficult to identify either in the archaeological record or in the pollen deposited in the lake sediments of the past. The clearances can be detected, and sometimes the pollen of maize (which is much larger than that of wild grasses) can be found, but there is not the same extensive clearance that has been recorded in Europe in prehistoric times. Populations were evidently smaller in North America and settlements were less permanent, so the environmental impact was less. There is evidence that forests were subjected to fire by Native American cultures, and often this led to a predominance of pine in some regions of North America. But it is very difficult in the dry climatic conditions of continental North America to distinguish between natural fires caused by lightning strikes and those lit by Native American peoples, who were using fire to clear areas for settlement or to smoke game animals out of hiding.

Despite these difficulties, one technique has recently been used successfully to trace the spread of maize cultivation from Mexico into the more northerly areas. This method depends on a chemical peculiarity of the maize plant. Maize belongs to a group of plants (called C4 plants) that photosynthesize in a slightly different way from most plants (called C3 plants), and this leaves an indelible record in the chemistry of their tissues. The animals that eat these plants also have the same record left in their bones, so we can tell when an animal has a large quantity of maize (or other C4 plant) in its diet by analyzing the chemistry of its fossil bones. By analyzing the bones of past human communities in North America, we can observe the first occurrence and the increasing dominance of maize in the diet and hence trace the spread of agriculture in this way. Another technique that allows archaeologists to follow the past use of crops from Central America, in this case root crops, such as yams (genus *Dioscorea*), cassava (*Manihot utilissima*), and arrowroot (*Maranta arundinacea*), is the microscopic examination of starch grains. There are subtle differences in the structure of the starch grains from these different crops, and they often survive as traces on the stone tools that were used for grinding the plant. So, it is possible to detect the arrival of agriculture and different crop species at different locations in North America.

In South America, evidence for the development and spread of agriculture can be detected in lake sediments, where forest clearance has resulted in rapid erosion of soils into lakes, and where charcoal from forest fires and pollen grains from crops and weeds testify to the changing landscape of former times. In the Andes of Peru, for example, there is evidence for extensive forest clearance and grassland spread about 4,000 years ago. Maize arrived in the area at about 100 C.E., but the predominant form of agriculture was pastoralism, using the llama as a domesticated grazing animal. Continued soil erosion silted up lakes and eventually led to the collapse of this prehistoric economy. At this time, around 1050 C.E., the Inca people spread through the region and the pollen record in the lakes shows that their arrival corresponded with an increase in alder trees. The Inca cultivated maize by developing terraces along the slopes in order to reduce soil erosion, and archaeologists believe that they also planted alder trees to assist in slope stability. This is one of the earliest records in the New World of landscape and agricultural conservation.

The idea of domestication, therefore, brought with it a need to modify vegetation, soils, and landscapes. The idea spread from the various centers where it had arisen, and domesticated plants and animals were transported far beyond the regions in which they had evolved. Climate imposed its own limits, determining how far north plants, such as maize, could grow and how high agriculture could be practiced in the mountains. In regions of extreme climate, different animals were domesticated, such as the caribou (reindeer) in Lapland and the yak in Tibet. In its inexorable spread, agriculture was to alter the whole face of the planet.

The origin of towns and cities

The domestication of animals and plants was a turning point in human history. Although disasters, such as flood, fire, drought, and disease, could still cause severe problems for the farmer, the presence of crops and herds of animals meant that the farmers were less vulnerable to famine than they had previously been. One outcome of the expansion of agriculture is that human populations began to grow. This is apparent both because of the increase in archaeological remains and also because of indirect evidence of environmental changes associated with people. The fossil pollen grains in lake sediments demonstrate that the oak forests of Syria, where early agriculture was developing, became more open in their structure and were gradually replaced by grasslands as the native population took to cultivation and the grazing of flocks. Humans had begun on the process of massive environmental modification.

Besides encouraging population growth, food surpluses also provided humans with more time for other activities.

The archaeological record displays a great increase in the diversity of artistic objects once the early farmers and herders had adopted agriculture. In the Sahara of North Africa, paintings have survived on rock outcrops that depict people and animals in great detail. Wild animals, including giraffe and elephant, are present, together with domesticated beasts, such as cattle. The artists were nomadic pastoralists who found time to record their activities on the rocks among which they camped. These nomadic herdsmen, like their modern counterparts in the drylands of the world, moved around with their animals, seeking areas of high plant productivity. Crop-raising people, however, could not move so freely from place to place; they needed to settle to raise and harvest their crops. A settled existence means that people can accumulate more belongings, including pots, tools, weapons, and decorative objects. So settlement can be regarded as an opportunity for technical innovation in tool manufacture and also for the development of art, social organization, and civilization.

Even the wandering pastoralists and the hunting people of the north built temporary camps, of course. The idea of residential camps was already established among such people as the mammoth hunters of Siberia, who built camps out of the bones and tusks of the mammoths they had killed. But the practice of agriculture demanded more extensive modification of the environment than hunting and gathering. Forests needed to be cleared and soils had to be dug over, and groups would want to stay at least several growing seasons to gain the benefits of all that effort. In time, the fertility of the soil would decline as successive crops were harvested, and it might become necessary to colonize new areas to maintain the productivity of the crop. But this might simply involve the clearing of an adjacent block of forest rather than moving any great distance, and the area that was left to recover could still be used for other purposes, such as dwellings or livestock housing, or even latrines and the disposal of waste. Such practices might well lead to the reuse of these plots for crop production at a later date, when the soil had become fertile once more. These conditions favored those who remained in one place for several years at a time. The pressure grew, therefore, to become settled rather than nomadic in lifestyle, particularly for those farmers involved in arable agriculture.

Thus, while pastoralists might still find a nomadic lifestyle appropriate, moving stock to new areas as old ones became depleted, in the Middle East the village became associated with cereal farming. Houses became more permanent. Flimsy structures of wood and mud became increasingly replaced by stone huts that required the investment of much time and effort; these would not be abandoned for many years. Stone-built constructions also survived through the centuries and have provided archaeologists with a record of early village life. In a typical hut, there was a central pole, and the roof over the rounded huts was constructed of reed thatch. Close to the middle of the hut would be a stone hearth, and the smoke from the fire would penetrate up through the loosely constructed roof. Sometimes burials, particularly of infants, took place beneath the floor of the hut, or special tombs were built that could contain several bodies. The burial of the dead in this way itself indicates a permanence of settlement. As a consequence of agriculture, the village had been born.

The Stone Age (Natufian) villages of Palestine, dating back to around 10,000 B.C.E., consisted of a few huts, perhaps only six in a group. This suggests that the village was made up of an extended family, or possibly several families, cooperating in farming an area of land, growing and harvesting crops, and herding animals. In addition to the bones of cattle and goats, the remains of such wild animals as gazelles, wild boars, hyenas, fish, tortoises, and snails show that hunting and foraging for food still played an important part in the diets of the inhabitants.

There probably developed a division of labor, a kind of specialization of activities. Evidence for this comes in part from the careful examination of skeletons associated with some more recent villages in Europe. Skeletons indicated that the females often suffered problems with their spines, hips, knees, and especially their toe joints, which were often swollen with arthritis. The reason for this was that women knelt upon the floor to grind the grain in the querns, bending their backs and putting strain on the bent toes of their feet. Male skeletons were usually free from these types of

problems but often have injuries associated with warfare or possibly the defense of herds from predators or bandits. This interpretation is confirmed by the occurrence of "female-type" bone problems in the skeletons of men who also had serious injuries, such as shattered limbs. These findings suggest that if a man was severely injured and could no longer follow the flocks, he would take on women's work and consequently suffered from the same types of bone problems.

This division of labor in the village may have become more elaborate as sophisticated skills were developed. The activities associated with later villages (tanning leather, working stone to make implements, making pottery, conducting religious activities, and, eventually, forging metals) all required skills and knowledge that are best achieved by individuals becoming specialists in their training and practice. But this degree of specialization of labor required larger communities to house all these skilled people, and the outcome was the town.

Excavations at Skara Brae on the island of Orkney, north Scotland, have revealed a prehistoric village preserved beneath deposits of blown sand. The houses in this late Stone Age village have hearths, beds, latrines, and covered passageways linking them to their neighbors. (Courtesy of George Metcalfe/ Peter D. Moore)

From village to town and city

One of the earliest towns to be discovered in the Middle East (indeed, one of the earliest towns in the world) is Jericho. Dating to around 7000 B.C.E., early Jericho had a series of round, mud-brick houses built on stone foundations, each of which had one to three rooms. In the middle of the town was a stone tower more than 25 feet (8 m) high, with an internal staircase, and around the perimeter of the town was a stone wall, five feet (1.6 m) thick and 13 feet (4 m) tall. Unlike the farming villages of the period, this was a fortified community, prepared to defend itself against attack from enemies. So here we find another reason why towns became necessary to these early farming cultures: defense. Within the town walls were storage systems for grain and water, possibly in preparation for any lengthy attack or siege. The tower was evidently the place of last resort, in case the enemy succeeded in breaking through the outer walls and invading the town. Then the residents could retreat to the final place of refuge and hope to hold out there. Such a fortified place of refuge (also known as a keep, donjon, or citadel) was a feature of towns and cities right up to the end of the Middle Ages just 500 years ago.

The growth of a town like Jericho suggests that the agricultural communities were now able to produce a surplus of food and produce beyond the needs of the individual families and villages. There was spare material that could be brought to centers of commerce, such as Jericho, and could be exchanged for specialist produce, such as woven cloth, tools, pottery, carpentry, or even luxury items, such as rings, brooches, or works of art. Archaeological excavation of Jericho has revealed a wealth of such objects. Agricultural surplus had led to the development of towns, and it was the origin of trading. It could also be argued that agricultural surplus was at the heart of artistic developments. Without an excess of foodstuffs and the consequent ability of some workers to spend their time in creative activity, both art and science would have been unable to develop, for everyone's hands would have been needed in the fields, from dawn to dusk. So the market town developed and grew into a city as the process of trade widened to become international in extent.

Just as domestication and agriculture arose in several different regions of the world, so did the development of the city. In the Middle East, towns and cities sprang up from the eastern Mediterranean to the valleys of the Tigris and Euphrates in modern-day Iraq. The valley of the Nile River was another focus for the development of civilization, extending up into the Ethiopian highlands. Farther east, the valley of the Indus River in modern Pakistan had a fertile agriculture, similar to that of the Nile and the Mesopotamian rivers, and developed its own urban civilization. There is evidence that these three regions were in trading contact with one another. More isolated was the civilization of the Far East, in the Yellow River region of what is now China, although trade routes existed that led west through the Gobi Desert and into Iran. Entirely separate from these, however, are the early civilizations of Central America and the Andes of Peru. Quite independently of the Old World, plant domestication and crop production

The village of Bhagestan in eastern Iran. Houses are built of mud and have rounded roofs. Barley grows in the surrounding fields, and the villagers also keep herds of sheep and goats. (Courtesy of Peter D. Moore)

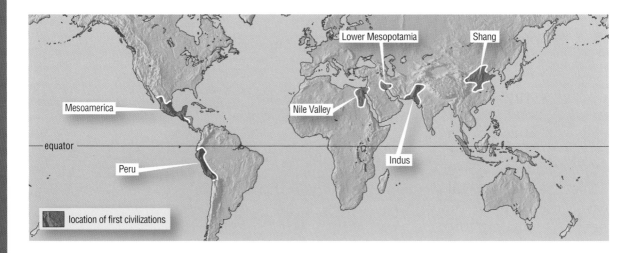

location of first civilizations

The areas where cities and civilizations first originated developed into an urban civilization in both of these centers. It seems that a general law of social evolution is being repeated here in different parts of the globe. Agriculture leads to the establishment of village settlements and villages grow into towns and cities.

Towns and cities, then, developed from villages, but not all villages developed into towns and cities. Why is this so? What factors led to a particular village expanding and changing its character in this way? The main answers seem to be defense and trade. A city was, by definition, a source of riches. Here the produce of the land was exchanged for valuable goods, perhaps even precious metals and stones or, in later times, coins. As a center of commercial activity, a city would attract the attention of anyone intent upon theft and robbery. So the city had to be able to defend itself by becoming established on a hilltop, with its back to a cliff, or with a river around one side. Not all villages were set in positions that could be well defended, so they were not suitable for development into larger towns and cities.

There are, however, exceptions to this rule. The early Mayan cities of Central America were rather different from those of Asia and Europe. They were much less compact, and there was a less clear distinction between the city and the country. In an analysis of an area of the ancient Mayan city of Landa, it was found that only 15 percent of the urban area was actually settled and occupied, so the city sprawled through the countryside. Perhaps this indicates a lack of need for defense against enemies. Most cities, however, were fortified, and this inevitably meant that they were compact and dense.

Being a center of trade and commerce, the city also needed to have good communications with surrounding areas, including other towns and cities. Jericho, for example, lay in the deep rift valley of the Jordan River, flowing from north to south into the Dead Sea and forming one of the main trade routes between ancient Assyria and Persia to the north and east, and Egypt to the south. Even before these ancient nations had come into being, in prehistoric times, Jericho occupied a commanding position through which people traveling either south or north had to pass. The inhabitants of Jericho, including the innkeepers, must have grown rich as they benefited from all the passing trade.

Within the growing population of the early cities, society became increasingly divided into groups, each having its own social status. This is apparent in the archaeological record because some homes and occupations are clearly richer than others. Researchers believe that a class structure emerged, including rich rulers, traders, skilled workers, lawyers, administrators, clerks, teachers, priests, and the laboring classes. In some cities an aristocratic class or even a royal family emerged, claiming a status above all others and a right to rule as a consequence of birth rather than ability. Some, such as the pharaohs of Egypt, some caesars in Rome, and the holy lords of the Mayan civilization of Central America, even claimed the status of gods. At the other end of the social scale were the slaves, people captured during raids on other cities or states, and these had a status only a little higher than the domestic animals.

In the early towns of the Middle East, scholars believe, this social structure, or caste system, was established by a tradition of debt or gift giving, that extended from the lowest to the most elite in society. It is a kind of taxation that ensured the increasing wealth of the leading people in a city. But this also led to the development of communal facilities within the city, which were financed from the riches of the leaders. Effectively, the city ruler or council imposed a tax upon all business conducted within the city, and this would have been used to build fortifications and to pay the army. Civilization and taxation, it seems, are inseparable. Tax revenue was also used to construct major monuments in the early cities and to support the building of temples and other religious structures. Each city developed its own characteristic buildings and statues that served to impress visitors and bring others to be impressed by its wonders. Temples, tombs, and pyramids were designed to become the wonders of the world and became the symbols of great cities and great rulers. Even today, cities pride themselves on certain buildings: museums, art galleries, statues, bridges, and so on. In this way the inhabitants of a city can proclaim its identity, importance, and civic pride. It is impossible, of course, to enter the minds of the people who belonged to these ancient civilizations and to determine precisely why they built their monuments, but the existence of civic grandeur is itself a testimony to the development of pride in their cities.

How many people actually inhabited early cities is difficult to calculate. Archaeological research indicates that the early Middle Eastern cities held between 7,000 and 20,000 people. The cities became rich because of their manufacturing industries and their trade. They grew because this wealth was attractive to rural dwellers and also because larger populations could be supported on the city's wealth. The movement of population from country to town is called *urbanization,* and it is a process that has continued to the present day. Urbanization has now begun to slow down or even reverse in the more developed nations, but it continues in many developing parts of the world. Some researchers into the evolution of cities have used the term *urban revolution* to describe the proliferation of cities in the ancient world, but like the agricultural revolution, it was a gradual process rather than a sudden one.

With the city came order and civilization; indeed, the words *city* and *civilization* come from the same root. A large community needs an organized structure, with a leader or a leading council of elders, a system of maintaining order and law, a defensive force or army, and a religious structure to provide moral guidance. It also turns its attention to developments in architecture and the arts. Very soon, the city would contain workers of all kinds except one. There were no farmers in the city, because farming was an activity associated with the open land and the village. There was no place for farms and farmers in the towns. So there developed a gulf in society between the town and the country dweller, and, to a large extent, this has been maintained right up to the present day.

Further evolution of cities

The earliest cities established a pattern of core attributes that still characterize cities today. These may be summarized as follows:

1. Cities are larger and more densely populated than villages.
2. They contain specialist activities and trade.
3. They are supported by the agriculture of surrounding areas.
4. They have monumental buildings and were often originally fortified.
5. They have a class structure within their populations.
6. They survive on trade.

As civilization developed and spread out from these centers of origin, the city still retained these features. But it also evolved new and sometimes complex characteristics that we associate with successful urban centers.

One such development was record keeping. As centers of commerce and government, cities had an interest in recording financial accounts and historical events. Writing itself is believed to have been invented in Mesopotamia, a highly bureaucratic and urban culture. The first Egyptian hieroglyphs arose at about the same time, around 3000 B.C.E. Translating these early inscriptions has been a long and difficult task for archaeologists, but the records of the early Egyptians and Mesopotamians can now be understood.

Another development associated with later cities is a growth in population. The rise of classical Greece was accompanied by the development of the great city of Athens. When its influence through the known world was at its height, around 500 B.C.E., it probably held about 150,000 citizens, together with around 20,000 foreigners living in the city and 100,000 slaves. Considering that the very largest of the earlier cities had only about 20,000 residents, the population of Athens was astronomical. This was the largest city that the world had ever seen, and its public buildings were proportionately grand and elaborate. On a hill in its center was the Acropolis, originally the fortified place of refuge of the early city. In more peaceful times the Acropolis developed into the hub of commercial, social, and political activity within the larger city. Around it were found the main council chambers, religious buildings, and the temples of the city, and radiating from it were the major roads, the trade arteries of the city.

Succeeding Athens as the greatest city of the ancient Western world was Rome. Rome was originally a collection of tribal settlements built on seven small hills and intersected by the Tiber River. This city rose to such prominence in the first few centuries C.E. that it effectively ruled much of the entire known world. The Tiber River led to the Mediterranean port of Ostia, and from there sea commerce could be maintained. With such a vast area of empire to support its activities, the city became exceedingly rich and attracted many inhabitants. It spread to cover around 5,000 acres (2,200 ha) and was built upon a central grid system with radiating roads leading out to the empire. The orderly planning of cities became a feature of Roman rule, and the grid system of streets was imposed upon all the new Roman cities of France, Spain, Germany, and Britain. This orderly and successful concept has continued right into modern times. Like Athens, Rome had a city center that featured municipal buildings, law courts, palaces, and a marketplace (the Forum). Rome was also a city in which leisure and recreation played important parts, and it was here at its heart that bathhouses, theaters, and the circus came to prominence as part of the provision of a great city for its inhabitants and visitors. The theater and the play as a source of entertainment had been an important element in Athenian culture, but in Rome the entertainment industry took on new proportions. The circus, for Rome, was an arena surrounded by tiers of seats from which such entertaining spectacles as chariot racing, battles between gladiators, and the execution of prisoners by wild beasts could be watched in comfort.

Public entertainment in the ancient world, however, was not restricted to the Mediterranean cultures. There is evidence that the Mayan civilization of Central America also indulged in elaborate public spectacles, particularly religious pageantry that could include human sacrifice. Music and dancing often accompanied religious ceremony, and archaeologists have also found evidence of team ball games. The importance of entertainment as a feature of the city has persisted to modern times.

Cities in medieval Europe developed along similar lines to those of Athens and Rome, but on a lesser scale. Often, the defensive requirements of these cities dominated the development of medieval European cities, so that a citadel, or keep, formed the center of the town. Around the keep was a highly developed area, the bailey, which was protected by strong outer walls and fortifications. The remainder of the city spread outside the walls and was far less well defended in times of war. The inhabitants of the outer city would seek refuge within the walls when threatened. (Many of the large cities of Europe have these structures still at their centers and have developed outward from this beginning. London is a good example, with the Tower of London, built in the 11th century, at its heart and the ancient city walls still intact in places, both now completely swallowed by the sprawl of a city that has consumed many of its surrounding satellite towns and converted them into suburbs.)

The industrial revolution brought the next major development to cities, starting in the 18th century. New urban areas grew up around the deposits of raw materials, such as coal, iron, and limestone, and these cities depended on the factories or the mines that were their source of employment and wealth. Residential and recreational facilities, such as they were, were packed in closely, so that the workers would not need to travel far to their work. Planners often used the traditional grid model, first developed by the Romans, which allowed high-density dwelling areas to be developed. Houses were linked together in terraces, all opening directly onto the street. There were no gardens at the front or the rear, but there were often small paved yards at the back, separated from one another by tall walls, and containing the family latrine. The industrial cities of Europe still contain some of these old developments, most of which have now been installed with modern facilities, such as running water, electricity, gas, and sewerage, but in some cities they have been replaced by high-rise buildings, in which even higher densities of population can be housed. The grid plan, however, has persisted. Indeed, it has proved particularly valuable in the days of motor transport, because it has greatly simplified major highway development and the extension of communication networks. Most North American cities developed or expanded after the invention of the automobile, so the grid system is very well established, while the cities of Europe were mainly initiated and developed before the existence of cars and have found it difficult to accommodate this form of transport within their irregular street patterns. Major reconstruction has often been required to provide for the needs of the motorist, and traffic congestion remains a common city problem.

Despite the successful innovations described here, the rise of civilization has not been a story of uninterrupted progress. Civilizations not only rise; they also fall. There are many reasons why cities may decline, but one important cause is the collapse of local agriculture. The Indus Valley civilization of Asia and the Mayan civilization of Central America both vanished at times of climatic change. Persistent drought accompanied the decline of these civilizations, cutting off the agricultural supply upon which they depended. Archaeologists have proposed the possibility that both civilizations also suffered from poor agricultural management in the dry conditions, and human failure to adapt to climatically stressful conditions undoubtedly contributed to the fall of these cultures. Recent evidence from the lake sediments of the Peruvian Andes also indicates that climatic dryness played an important part in the decline of the Inca civilization. The eastern Mediterranean center of civilized development may well have survived because of its spread into Europe and North Africa, which allowed it to survive the climatic aridity that also affected that part of the world. As noted previously, cities are supported by and dependent upon the agriculture of their surrounding areas. If the local agricultural production fails, then the city begins to starve; its population falls, and its trade and wealth consequently decline.

Conclusions

The domestication of wild plants and animals provided humans with an assured source of food. People adapted their natural environment in such a way that their crops and their livestock became more productive. They cleared forest, plowed soils, and created grasslands for their domestic plants and animals, and they reaped the reward of an assured supply of food. The idea of agriculture arose independently in several different parts of the world, from China to Central America. In each area the plants and animals available for domestication were different, and in some areas, such as Europe, these domestic organisms were taken far beyond their original biogeographic ranges.

Towns and cities were built upon the produce of agriculture. Without the surplus of food produced as a consequence of agricultural development, the city could never have evolved. Cities have developed because of increasing specialization of skills and roles in society among their inhabitants. Society in cities became layered, with the lower social levels donating produce or money to higher levels, so that ruling classes emerged. From this structure, finance became available for the support of armies and the building of monuments and fortifications. Like agriculture, the city also had many geographical origins in different parts of the world, and with the city came civilization. In the course of time, some of these civilizations have declined or died, sometimes as a consequence of changing climate, but others have survived and have led to the cities that we know today. Just like the ancient cities, modern cities are still sustained by agriculture and trade.

CHAPTER 6

AGRICULTURAL AND URBAN CONSERVATION

Farms and cities exist primarily for human use. They are our habitat and people take priority within them. Unlike our national parks, where wildlife is often given the pride of place and human activities come second to the needs of wild plants and animals, in cities and farmland human needs are placed first. Humans require a healthy environment, so all animals that present a threat to health, such as rats, mosquitoes, and pathogenic bacteria, must be discouraged in cities. In farmland the production of high-quality food for human consumption is the priority, and all animals and pest plants that interfere with this process, from deer to aphids, may find themselves unwelcome. So biodiversity can never be the prime aim of the farmer or the city dweller.

On the other hand, the quality of life in the city and the quality of food productivity on the farm can be accompanied by a wealth of wildlife that is at worst harmless and at best even beneficial to these aims. Trees cast shade and produce oxygen that improves air quality; the sound of birds singing can calm the nerves; grassland and lawns encourage recreation; and landscaped parks inspire the imagination. Sharing our cities with wildlife, therefore, can be of immediate benefit to people. Similarly, in farmland, biodiversity can bring great advantages. Areas of apparently unproductive land provide habitats for the predators of pest insects. Ladybugs, for example, can find a permanent habitat in rough grassland from which they move out into crops and consume aphid pests. In many respects, a farmland with high biodiversity is likely to prove a healthy one.

The value of biodiversity

Cities and agricultural land occupy large areas of the Earth's land surface, and they contain a considerable variety of wild plants and animals that have managed to adapt to these types of habitats. They are relatively new habitats in geological terms, having existed for only about 10,000 years, but wild animals and plants have changed their behavior patterns and evolved new characteristics that have equipped them for a new lifestyle alongside people. Farms and cities are therefore quite biodiverse, and this is a feature that humans may want to retain or even enhance.

People benefit from some undomesticated plants and animals. Trees, for example, grow in most cities. Some of these trees may be native to the region and others are often imported from other parts of the world. Why do people plant trees, thus using up valuable space in cities where offices, factories, or homes could be built? One answer is that they are useful. Trees carry out photosynthesis, a process in which they manufacture sugars out of the carbon dioxide in the atmosphere. At the same time they produce oxygen as a waste product. It so happens that we humans and the machines we use do precisely the opposite. We take in oxygen in our respiration and we expel carbon dioxide. So the trees are recycling our waste products and producing the oxygen that we need to survive. In hot, sunny climates, trees are also valuable for the shade that they cast. The palm trees of Los Angeles, California, the pine and plane trees of Tehran, Iran, and the banyan of the Indian village all provide a welcome shelter from the heat of the sun. Trees can thus change the microclimate, creating cooler conditions by reflecting back some of the sunlight. Trees also absorb sound. An avenue of trees or shrubs between a highway and residential or office buildings is one of the most effective types of noise barriers that is available. The pockets of air that are held between the twigs and leaves of trees act as a kind of muffling device that soaks up sound.

But trees are welcome in cities not just because they are useful but also because they are decorative. Indeed, we sometimes choose to plant exotic trees in our cities because we find them beautiful or interesting. So part of the benefit we gain from trees in cities relates to our enjoyment in being surrounded by living things, particularly beautiful living things. When we encourage biodiversity in our cities and farms, therefore, we may do so because other species of plants and animals are useful, or simply because we enjoy having them there. Both arguments can be used in favor of biodiversity enhancement.

Farmers and city dwellers alike should be concerned about maintaining biodiversity because we never know when we will need to use other animals and plants for the benefit of our species. In agriculture, for example, we presently depend on just a few plants and animals for our food (see "Domesticated plants and animals," pages 106–110). As food production becomes increasingly important for our survival, we will undoubtedly have to look for new species that we can bring into domestication. There are still grasses in such regions as Mexico and Syria that have the capacity to grow in dry conditions or where the soils are saline, and these species and varieties have much to offer us in the improvement of our grain-producing crops. The development of techniques for genetic manipulation has made it easier to move genes from one species to another. In case we need to draw upon them in the future, therefore, the genetic resources of our wild plants need careful protection.

Wild species also have potential chemical and health applications. Some plants contain toxic chemicals that they have developed to deter grazing animals, but many of these toxins have important medical applications. Certain species of bean, for example, are a source of the drug that is used to treat Parkinson's disease. Screening plants for their drug potential is an important area of research, and it is important that wild species and varieties should not become extinct before their properties are known. If farms were to occupy the whole face of the Earth, there would be no habitats left where wild plants could survive, and we would never be able to make use of them as sources of food or medicine.

Some of the organisms that share our cities likewise deserve conservation because of their potential value. The grasses that inhabit urban sites, for example, have often developed a tolerance to some of the toxic gases emitted in smoke and from automobile exhausts. Sulfur dioxide is one of these gases, and grasses that have long been exposed to this gas are often capable of survival in extremely polluted environments. Similarly, several of the common weeds that invade our lawns and roadsides, including the plantains, have become highly tolerant of lead pollution as a result of exposure to this metal in exhaust fumes. Tolerance to toxins can be very useful because plants that have this capacity can be used to reclaim heavily contaminated sites and provide the first stage in a process called *remediation,* the repair of badly damaged habitats.

How can wild species be conserved? One way is to assemble collections of animals and plants in captivity, where they can be cared for and protected from the dangers and diseases they may face in the wild. Zoological parks and botanical gardens are often located in our major cities, so in this way the city has become a focus of biodiversity conservation. In times past the zoo functioned mainly as a place of entertainment for the inhabitants of cities or, at best, as a place for education. Most zoos now have adopted the more responsible task of conservation and concentrate on captive breeding programs of threatened species with the intention of reintroduction into the wild. Botanical gardens have often originated as collections of plants destined for horticulture. Like zoos, they have also served as places of recreation. But they, too, have increasingly become centers of scientific research and plant conservation. Plants can be stored, often for long periods, as seeds, and the construction of seed banks has become a particularly valuable means of plant conservation. Seeds are kept in dry, cold conditions and are periodically germinated, grown to maturity, and allowed to flower so that seed stocks can be replenished. Like the zoo, the botanical garden now takes on a protective function, a backup in case disaster causes the elimination of wild populations of plants. This role will prove particularly important in the preservation of different varieties of crop plants that may have become less popular than formerly and are in danger of being lost.

Conservation of biodiversity, then, brings benefits, by maintaining useful and aesthetically pleasing species in our urban and agricultural environments. In our urban zoos and botanical gardens we have an important opportunity for practicing this conservation.

Increasing biodiversity in cities and farms

Conserving biodiversity means protecting the range of plants and animals around us and making sure that they are not lost. But we can go further than this; we can create conditions in which biodiversity flourishes, and thus increase biodiversity.

There are two main factors in both cities and farmland that operate against biodiversity: fragmentation and uniformity of habitats. As discussed previously, both of these features affect organisms found in these habitats (see "Patterns of development," pages 11–15). Fragmentation involves the breaking of habitats into smaller and smaller pieces, which results in fewer species being able to occupy them. In the case of forest, for example, both farm and city development involve clearance, often in patches, leaving small blocks of forest that decrease in size as the development continues. The distances between the remaining fragments also become greater so that animals and plants isolated in these fragments may find it difficult to maintain contact with other populations of the same species, and this can have a number of different biological effects.

Uniformity of habitat is another feature of many parts of the city and of some agricultural landscapes. The main central commercial regions of cities are often dominated by bare concrete, and some of the most productive of our wheat-producing regions may consist of seemingly endless monocultures of a single plant species.

Increasing biodiversity involves maintaining areas for wildlife conservation that are as big as possible and are relatively close together or are linked by corridors. It also demands that habitats should be made that are as varied as possible, thus avoiding the uniformity that humans so often create. In the case of farms, for example, the use of a mixed farming system (including both arable and pastoral activities) serves to increase biodiversity. Livestock grazing in a meadow prevents the grassland becoming dominated by just a few species of aggressive grasses or shrubs. This means that a greater variety of plants can grow, including some smaller ones that occupy the closely grazed or trampled patches. The grazers affect the structure of the grassland; cows create tussocky meadows, whereas sheep produce a more uniform short turf.

The meadowlark species (*Sturnella magna* and *S. neglecta*) provide a useful illustration of what is needed if biodiversity is to be conserved or even increased. Meadowlarks are most at home in open, grazed grassland, nesting in tussocks of grass where they can obtain some cover for the nest from surrounding vegetation. They feed upon insects, such as grasshoppers, and use fence posts for perching. But they also use arable land, particularly in the fall when they feed on grain and weed seeds. They need the grassland for their nests but can manage if strips of grass are maintained alongside the fields. A diversity of habitats is needed to maintain a population of meadowlarks, so a farming system that becomes too uniform is likely to lose this species, and many others with it.

Even the choice of crop, or the manner in which crops are farmed can influence biodiversity. If winter wheat (which is sown in the fall) is used instead of spring-sown wheat, then stubble fields, together with their weed seeds, will not be present through the winter and meadowlarks will find themselves deprived of this resource. The increase in planting winter wheat may be one of the factors underlying the falling numbers of songbirds in America and in Europe. The excessive use of pesticides is another factor in this decline because it reduces the insect food available to birds.

Increasing the diversity of habitats increases the diversity of wildlife (including both plants and animals) in the city as well as in the countryside. People cultivate gardens in the city principally for aesthetic enjoyment of the cultivated plants, together with the wild animals, such as birds and butterflies, attracted by them. But a city garden can also be designed to enhance biodiversity by creating a range of habitats. Trees and shrubs provide shelter and feeding sites for insectivorous birds, such as warblers, while lawns attract ground feeders, like the American robin. Water in a garden is a sure way of gaining biodiversity because water is often a scarce resource in a city, especially during long dry summers. We can, of course, supplement the food supply for visiting birds by erecting bird feeders, and we can even provide breeding opportunities by constructing nest boxes. Feeding birds is an excellent way of increasing the diversity and the density of birds in our gardens, but only if food is supplied consistently. Birds soon come to rely on a source of food and may find themselves in difficulties if it suddenly disappears. Also, the food must be the right type to provide a healthy diet for local species. Some birds, like starlings and crows, are omnivorous and will take anything on offer, from meat scraps to bread. For many garden birds, however, such as house finches (*Carpodacus mexicanus*), a range of different seeds provides a more attractive and healthy diet. House finches living on a poor diet change color; they lose their bright red breasts and foreheads and become a dull yellow color. Sunflower seeds and peanuts are particularly rich in oil and are therefore a good source of energy, but they must be in good condition. Fungi will infect seeds that have been stored in damp locations, and this can cause disease and death in the birds that feed on them.

Promoting city biodiversity involves tradeoffs, however. For example, pesticides protect garden plants from insects that damage them, increasing the growth and biodiversity of city plants. But destroying these insects deprives the organisms that depend on them as a food supply, such as birds. Worse, the pesticide may poison animals that eat tainted insects. Some insecticides are based on plant products containing chemicals evolved by the plants as a means of deterring plant-feeding insects. Insecticides of this kind are least harmful to birds and other insect eaters. Any pesticide used must have a very short lifespan in the environment to protect insectivores. To best protect the biodiversity of animals, the answer is to avoid the use of pesticides completely, but of course doing so leaves plants vulnerable. Encouraging biodiversity has its cost.

People and wildlife

The relationship between people and wildlife is complicated, and especially so in cities and farms. We eat plants and animals. In a farm setting this is the dominant aspect of our relationship, and we have to protect the plants and animals we eat from predators, pests, and parasites. In the town we are less aware of our need for plants and animals as food because we obtain them wrapped in plastic from the store. Both in the city and in the country we also generally enjoy wildlife. We may be unique among the living organisms on Earth in having an aesthetic interaction with wildlife, being mentally uplifted and refreshed by the presence of other organisms. Termites, together with some beetles and ants, build gardens for food production (equivalent to our agriculture), but no other animal builds gardens simply for the enjoyment of beauty. The biological function of the flower is to attract a pollinator, but we find flowers attractive and stimulating even though we have no intention of pollinating them. Our attitude toward wildlife is often an extension of our regard for decorative flowers in our gardens, but wildlife is more than simply decorative in the human perception. We may even keep pets not for any practical purpose (work animals such as sheepdogs, packhorses, elephants, and camels serve in this respect) but simply for company and amusement.

We like to see wild birds, butterflies, and plants in our surroundings, and we benefit from these. Human health is often closely related to our mental state. It is widely recognized that a stressed and troubled lifestyle has physical impacts upon our bodies, contributing to conditions that range from stomach ulcers to heart disease. Stress can also lead people to take up unhealthy habits, such as cigarette smoking, excessive alcohol consumption, and taking other drugs as a source of relief. The use of animals in some hospitals as a means of relaxation and mental stimulation demonstrates how other species can be therapeutic to humans. If wildlife can reduce stress, then it is clearly a valuable source of medical assistance.

There are some animals, however, that pose a threat to human welfare and that cannot be accommodated within the city. In parts of North America, such as San Diego, the mountain lion is proving a menace by attacking pet dogs and cats, and even threatening human life on occasion. The problem is largely due to the loss of the mountain lion's natural habitat as a result of agricultural and housing development, so people are ultimately responsible for this human/mountain lion interaction. But there is clearly a limit to the extent of wildlife biodiversity that can be maintained within the city. Some animals and plants may interfere with our lives to such an extent that they become regarded as pests.

The human need for rural elements even within the heart of cities led to the development of parks and open spaces in city planning. London, England, for example, developed much of its present form between 1775 and 1850, when new developments of residential housing were being erected on the north side of the Thames River. The main style of development was in "squares." These were not blocks of the North

American variety, but open sites with grass and trees surrounded by terraces of tall (usually four-story) buildings. The residents of the buildings thus had open areas for recreation and also had semirural views from their front windows. These squares still form a feature of central London, and many form havens for wildlife deep within the city. A similar approach has been used more recently in Toronto, Canada, where residential courtyards can be shared by the occupants of the houses surrounding them, and these are accompanied by neighborhood parks and urban squares that are open to the wider public. Larger parks with greater wildlife potential, such as Regents Park in London, Central Park in New York, the Commons in Boston, Massachusetts, and Mount Royal in Montreal, Canada, represent attempts to bring a rural landscape into the center of cities. They enrich the cityscape in a visual way, but they also provide a means of relaxation and stress management. Rural patches in cities are constructed as a recognition that human beings are refreshed and stimulated by such landscapes, as well as by the wildlife they contain. In more recent years, with skyrocketing urban land prices, city planners have tended to neglect this approach, substituting smaller and more formal arrangements of gardens and trees. Though cheaper and still attractive, these are less effective as a means of wildlife conservation.

While parks and gardens supply a welcome relief within the city, derelict land is usually regarded as an unwanted feature. Human taste is complex; while appreciating wildlife, we tend not to enjoy disorder and untidiness, so we prefer to create habitats in which the human hand is evident. Wasteland nonetheless has value as a refuge for wildlife. Vacant land provides at least a temporary opportunity for wildlife to occupy locations within cities. In modern cities there are often temporary vacant lots, but these are economically unproductive so are rapidly developed. They do, however, form an important habitat for the itinerant plants and animals that can rapidly complete their life cycles and move on to the next available site. Some of the most successful wildlife of the city is essentially nomadic.

In the countryside the creation of landscapes by people is also an important aspect of conservation. All landscapes are mosaics, constructed of intricate arrangements of patches of different scales. The natural landscape rarely contains straight lines or regular arrangements of objects. This suits most people's taste; people generally dislike uniformity and too rigid a regularity. Those features that we find attractive in towns are also the ones we appreciate in the country, variety and a certain degree of irregularity. Perfectly geometric fields, straight boundaries and right angles are less pleasing to the eye than the irregular patchwork of fields that has resulted from the piecemeal development of our more ancient areas of settlement and farming. It so happens that irregular mosaics also favor a high diversity of animal and plant

Central Park, New York, in winter. Patches of relatively natural habitats in the centers of cities offer urban inhabitants recreational opportunities. Parks also provide habitats for urban wildlife. (Courtesy of Bart Parren)

species, hence human aesthetic preferences can promote biodiversity.

The demands of modern agriculture for productivity and economic sustainability have led to larger fields and the loss of irregular patchworks in our landscape. Small fields with irregular boundaries are difficult to manage with modern farm machinery. These changes in field size and shape have had an adverse impact on the habitat diversity and the biodiversity of our countryside. Farmers' prime responsibility is to supply an ever-increasing demand for food. High productivity requires intensive farming, and this inevitably leads to reduced biodiversity. It is possible to preserve the small scale and irregularity of old farmland, but doing so costs money. Farmers need to make a living, and smaller fields are economically inefficient. If they are required to neglect parts of their land in the interests of wildlife conservation, it is only fair to compensate farmers for lost income. Britain is attempting to do just that. A system known as *set-aside* has been introduced, in which farmers are paid by the government to leave parts of their land uncultivated for a number of years, thus providing new wildlife habitats. This may seem contrary to all the aims of agriculture, but organized wildlife conservation such as this will become increasingly necessary if we are to avoid a great loss of our wild plants and animals. The patches of unused land in our agricultural landscapes also have a certain economic value, because they provide refuges for many useful insects and birds, particularly the ones that prey upon the pests of crops.

The adoption of new crops, new plant varieties, and new methods of farming is also affecting our wildlife. For instance, winter wheat (sown in the fall) has largely replaced spring-sown wheat, with the result that fields once bare through the winter and a source of seeds to wild birds are now occupied by growing plants. Many rural birds, including the meadowlark, have lost a source of winter feed. This change has also had an impact on urban bird populations because many city birds spend their winter in surrounding farmlands where they can find a source of food in waste grain and weed seeds. Like human city dwellers, urban birds remain dependent on surrounding farmland for their support. There has been a decline in the population of many urban birds in recent years, and this may well be a result of what farmers would regard as cleaner and more efficient use of their land and resources.

One form of wildlife people have gone to great pains to outsmart is the group of plants we know as weeds. But ever since agriculture began, weeds have evolved to match crops and have thus maintained farmland biodiversity. For example, many of the most successful weeds in the past have been those that are harvested with the crop and then sown with the crop in the following year. This is best achieved if the seed of the weed is the same size as the seed of the crop, because farmers have long practiced winnowing, in which the grain is cast into the air and the different sizes of seed are separated according to their weights. Heavy seeds fall close to their source while small seeds travel farther. A weed seed that closely resembled the grain in size and weight would prove difficult to separate and would be effectively dispersed for its next season of growth. So the method used historically by the farmer to eliminate weeds actually placed an evolutionary selection on their development. While screening methods were simple, nature managed to keep pace with human technology and biodiversity was maintained. During the last century, however, seed screening has become much more sophisticated and efficient, so that many of the weeds that once accompanied our crops are disappearing from the countryside.

The relationship between people and wildlife in both city and farmland, then, is a complex one. We like to share our environment with some species, but in the interests of health, safety, and the productivity of our crops and domestic animals, we wish to eliminate other species. Many of the developments occurring within cities and farms, from intensive urban development to factory farming, militate against biodiversity in either habitat. But there is also a degree of pleasure to be obtained from a biodiverse environment, whether it is in an urban garden or a country landscape, so we must balance economic advancement against the less easily measured advantages of human satisfaction and comfort.

Conserving domesticated breeds

The development of new varieties of a crop plant can increase productivity, so agriculturalists have been breeding new strains of crops and domestic animals ever since agriculture began. The farm has always been a hotbed of evolution as farmers selected certain individuals with high-quality attributes and bred from them. Breeding plants and animals to ensure that they are both productive and highly adapted to environmental conditions has resulted in a diversity of forms of our cultivated plants and domesticated animals.

This diversity is in danger of being lost because specialized breeds may be expensive to maintain. Often they are highly efficient in a very limited range of extreme conditions. For example, a strain of barley may be capable of withstanding intense drought or high salinity or poor nutrient conditions in the soil. Such a variety may be resistant to such stresses, but it will probably be less productive than other strains. There is a danger that breeding highly productive strains of crops will lead to their universal adoption even in regions where occasional stresses, such as drought, can lead to crop failure. If the more specialized strains are lost, then the genetic variability of that crop species will be lost with them, and agriculture as a whole will be poorer. This is a particular danger in a world where plant breeding takes place on an industrial scale and the international distribution of a new variety can lead to its rapid establishment around the world, even in developing regions where local breeds may have better long-term prospects of survival. It is important that we should conserve the biodiversity of our domesticated species as well as the diversity of wildlife on our farms.

One recent development in crop and domestic animal breeding that has become a source of controversy is genetic modification. In a sense, we have been genetically manipulating plants and animals ever since agriculture began, for we have been selective in our breeding programs to ensure the persistence of the particular features we require. In genetic engineering the long slow process of selection and natural breeding can be cut short. The genes that control a particular feature (such as full grain, salt tolerance, insect resistance, or early flowering) can be located on the DNA strands, cut out, and incorporated into the genetic material of a receptor plant. Usually bacteria are used to transport and inject the new nucleic acid. The process allows the operator to be very specific about the alterations to be carried out, and is also extremely fast when compared to conventional breeding programs.

The consequences of genetic modification of crops are strongly debated among environmentalists, however. Some feel that such developments carry serious risks, such as the possibility that genes controlling herbicide resistance that could be introduced into crop plants could then escape into wild plant populations and produce "superweeds." These would prove impossible to control using standard herbicides. On the other hand, if we could increase general pest resistance among our crops, then less pesticide would be needed and the environment could become cleaner. Genetic modification also raises ethical questions, such as whether we have a right to take genes from one organism and translate them into another, possibly of a different species. The issue stirs a degree of public discomfort. Some people also point out that the long-term effects of food products derived from genetically modified organisms are not known. (If the chemistry of the product is identical to that of conventional food, however, there is little risk associated with its consumption.) Many people fear that genetic manipulation will result in some terrible outcome, a modern-day Frankenstein's monster. Today's challenge is to support the widest possible biodiversity among our domesticated species. We can accomplish this aim both by conserving the array of historically important breeds and by improving future domesticated stocks through the responsible use of modern methods.

Climate change

We know that climate is currently changing quite rapidly. Over the past 150 years, the world's temperature has risen by almost 3°F (1.5°C). Determining what has caused this change is complex because the climate is constantly changing, even without human assistance, and the cold conditions of the little Ice Age that began in the 13th century have clearly come to an end since around 1850.

Nonetheless, most climatologists agree that the change has also been influenced by human activities on the planet. In particular, we have produced large quantities of carbon dioxide by burning fossil fuels, and the rising levels of this gas in the atmosphere (which are now well documented) have led to more heat retention by the atmosphere, a phenomenon known as the "greenhouse effect." But in addition, changes in land use and the development of cities have had a direct impact on the climate. A recent study of climate trends across North America has shown that the greatest rises in temperature have been concentrated in the eastern and in the western areas, with little change (or even a slight fall) in the Midwest. The greatest overall change is due to a rise in the minimum temperatures, and the development of cities has undoubtedly contributed to this warming trend. Cities radiate heat at night, and this has influenced the climate of whole regions. It is reckoned that 0.5°F (0.27°C) of the temperature rise over the last 100 years has been a consequence of urbanization and land-use change.

Towns affect the regional climate, but climate can also affect the towns. Within the next 50 years we can expect higher summer temperatures that will often bring drought. This means that there will be an increasing demand for water to irrigate parks and gardens. Some of the plants currently grown may prove unsuitable and planners will have to look to drought-resistant trees in regions where this is not yet a problem. Increased temperature will mean increased energy consumption for air-conditioning, although the winter heating demands may decrease. City wildlife may also change as species extend their ranges northward. Already we have seen the Indian rose-ringed parakeet (*Psittacula krameri*) has invaded Los Angeles, New York, and London, and we can expect to see further expansions in the range of tropical and subtropical species that can live alongside humans in cities.

Changing climate is expected to be accompanied by rising world sea levels, and this will have a strong impact on cities around the globe. Vancouver, Canada; Seattle, Washington; San Francisco and Los Angeles, California; Miami, Florida; New York; and Boston, Massachusetts, are just a few of the cities that will be placed under stress if the sea level rises by around two feet (65 cm), which could happen within 80 years. This event will raise a huge civil engineering problem: the need to build flood-protection barriers to prevent the inundation of the low-lying areas of our cities.

The consequences of climate change for farmland is even more serious. We can expect to see shifts in the zones of agriculture over much of North America. The United States breadbasket, for example, which currently lies south and west of the Great Lakes region, will move significantly north and east if the temperature rises by an additional degree or two. Cereal growing will become increasingly difficult in the south of the current range but will become more efficient in Michigan and Wisconsin. In southern Canada a further substitution of winter wheat for spring wheat is likely to result, with consequent wildlife implications. Cereal yields are likely to decline in Mexico and in parts of South America, such as Argentina and Uruguay. In sub-Saharan Africa, crop productivity is already strongly affected by variations in rainfall from year to year, and as rainfall may well become even more erratic, yields may fall. Grain yields in the more southerly countries of Africa, such as Zimbabwe, will also fall if the global temperature continues to rise. In Southeast Asia the staple crop, rice, is dependent on irrigation, so any change in monsoon rainfall to this area or to the Himalayas, which act as a water-gathering region for the lowland plains, could make rice cultivation more difficult. Additionally, Bangladesh and other parts of Southeast Asia are low-lying and will suffer from rising sea levels as well as the direct impact of climate change. The Pacific islands will also be badly affected by sea-level rise.

Climate change will also affect weeds and insect pests. In general, it is the hotter parts of the world that suffer most from pests affecting food production and food storage, so rising temperature is bad news from this point of view. Insects are cold-blooded and any rise in temperature means that they can grow faster, move more quickly, and breed more rapidly. We can expect to see an upsurge in insect pests as a result of global warming. Aphids (plant-sucking insect pests), for example, will grow and reproduce faster in the spring and may reach plague proportions under warmer conditions. We may also expect more frequent population explosions among locusts in drier regions. Some pests winter in the southern areas and move northward each spring. The potato leafhopper, for example, currently spends its winter in Florida and along the coastal fringe of the Gulf of Mexico. Global warming is predicted to permit this pest to spend the winter farther north in Louisiana, Mississippi, and Alabama, thus enabling it to invade the northern regions more rapidly each spring.

The overall picture regarding agriculture and climate change is a negative one. Higher world temperatures may mean that we can grow grain farther north, but the regions closer to the equator will suffer reduced productivity and greater losses to pests. This will impact particularly severely on developing nations in the tropics and subtropics, where food production is already under strain. For example, more than 60 percent of the population of sub-Saharan Africa is involved in farming, and climate change will hit this region particularly severely. Although the rich, developed nations will be able to cope with the agricultural changes associated with a warmer climate, it is undoubtedly true that the poorer countries will suffer most.

Global populations and the future

There are currently more than 6 billion people on Earth, and, as noted in the introduction to this book, this number may well rise to 10 billion by 2025. An increasing proportion is resident in cities, where there are more employment opportunities than in the surrounding countryside. The question is whether the countryside can support the cities with continuing food supplies into the future. It is possible to extend agriculture farther over the land surface of the Earth, but there is limited opportunity here and any further destruction of natural habitats will reduce biodiversity. Through such agricultural expansion we could lose the very species that will provide the food, drugs, building materials, and genetic resources that we will need to preserve our species into the following century. The biome that we have created in urban and agricultural ecosystems is rapidly coming to dominate the world, and it is possible that all other biomes will eventually be represented by small fragments of natural habitat preserved in national parks. The loss of the world's wilderness seems almost inevitable.

Mass of pedestrians, Amritsar, India. It is calculated that the global human population will have reached 10 billion by 2025. (Courtesy of Mitsuaki Iwago/ Minden Pictures)

There is a limit to human population levels, determined ultimately by the Earth's limited resources, and we must be rapidly approaching it. The question we need to ask is what factors will ultimately stabilize world population: natural biological processes of disease and starvation, the behavioral response of warfare, or the rational self-limitation of further population growth? The biome that we have ourselves created in the last 10,000 years could so easily run out of control, swallow all of the others, and then self-destruct. We can only hope that reason wins through and that such a catastrophe is averted.

Conclusions

Biodiversity is one of Earth's most precious resources, and it is in people's best interests to ensure that it is not lost or wasted. Even in cities and farmlands, biodiversity can still be high, but only if we resist the demands of high-density dwelling and high-intensity agricultural production, both of which diminish biodiversity. Both cities and farms can be made attractive to wildlife if we maintain a mosaic of landscapes within each. There are fragments of habitats remaining in our cities, in the form of parks, waterways, and gardens, and these can support wildlife, especially if people create the microhabitats needed for breeding and supply additional support in the form of food. In the countryside we need to encourage small fields, diverse hedges and grass verges, patches of neglected land, and woodlots. Wildlife can adjust to land-use changes and new crops, but evolution is relatively slow, and the techniques of rapid crop development now in use may outpace natural evolution and lead to the extinction of some familiar species.

The climate is changing and this will also affect cities and farms. Many of the great cities of the world lie close to sea level and will be badly affected as the sea level rises. Plants grown in gardens today may no longer be suitable as conditions become hotter and possibly drier, and gardeners will have to substitute different species. The crops that farmers grow will also change, and some crops will be grown farther north than formerly. City and farm wildlife will likewise change in response to alterations in climate.

The urban and agricultural biome is a human creation. We have taken 10,000 years to construct it, but it is now changing more rapidly than ever before in its history. The human population is growing at an unprecedented rate, and it will soon exceed the capacity of the farmland to supply enough food. Farmland can expand only into areas where the climatic conditions favor crop growth or animal grazing, so even if we allow our biome to engulf all others, opportunity for further expansion is very limited. By the natural laws of population ecology, the resources of the planet will finally limit our numbers. The Earth has a carrying capacity for people that will undoubtedly be reached within the present century; indeed, it may have been reached already. The future of the urban and agricultural biome lies in our own hands, and with it lies the future of all the other biomes.

GLOSSARY

acid rain precipitation made acidic by the air pollutants produced by industrial activity

adobe mud bricks that have been baked by the heat of the Sun rather than in an oven, or a structure built of such bricks

adsorption the loose attachment of an element or ion upon a soil particle, such as clay

agriculture the cultivation of land for the production and exploitation of plants (arable) and animals (pastoral)

albedo an index that relates to the degree of reflectivity of a surface to light. Snow has a high albedo, while dark-colored vegetation has a low albedo

anaerobic lacking oxygen (= anoxic)

anion elements or groups of elements carrying a negative charge, such as NO_3^-, HPO_3^-

annual an organism (usually a plant) that completes its life history in a single year

anoxic lacking oxygen (= anaerobic)

arable describing land cultivated for the growing of domesticated plants

aspect the direction of the compass that a slope faces

biocontrol *see* BIOLOGICAL CONTROL

biodiversity the full range of living things found in an area, together with the variety of genetic constitutions within those species and the range of habitats available at the site

biogeography the scientific study of the spatial distribution of living animals and plants

biological control the use of an organism, usually a parasite, pathogen, or predator, to control the population of a pest species

biomass the quantity of living material within an ecosystem, including those parts of living organisms that are part of them but are strictly nonliving (such as wood, hair, teeth, or claws) but excluding separate dead materials on the ground or in the soil (termed *litter*)

biosphere those parts of the Earth and its atmosphere in which living things are able to exist

blue-green bacteria (cyanobacteria)   microscopic, colonial, photosynthetic microbes, which are able to fix nitrogen; once wrongly called blue-green algae. They play important ecological roles in some wetlands as a consequence of this nitrogen-fixing ability, such as in rice paddies

bluff body   a rounded or irregularly shaped structure, which obstructs wind flow patterns; the opposite of a streamlined form

bog   a wetland ecosystem in which the water supply is entirely from rainfall. Such wetlands are acidic and poor in nutrient elements. They accumulate a purely organic peat with very little mineral matter (derived solely from airborne dust), so are prized for horticulture

boreal   northern, usually referring to the northern temperate regions of North America and Eurasia, which are typically vegetated by evergreen coniferous forests and wetlands. Named after Boreas, the Greek god of the north wind

browsing   the activity of a vertebrate herbivore feeding upon trees and shrubs

calcareous   rich in calcium carbonate (lime)

capillaries   fine tubelike air spaces found in the structure of partially compacted soils

capillarity   the tendency of water to move along capillaries, even against the force of gravity, as a consequence of its surface tension forces

carbon sink   an ecosystem that absorbs more carbon from the atmosphere than it releases in respiration. Some wetland habitats operate in this way

catchment   a region drained by a stream or river system (equivalent to the term *watershed*)

cation   an element or group of elements with a positive charge, such as Na^+, NH_4^+, or Ca^{++}

cation exchange   the substitution of one positively charged ion for another. Certain materials (such as peat and clay) have the capacity to attract and retain cations and to exchange them for hydrogen in the process of leaching

chamaephyte   a plant that grows close to the surface of the ground, below a height of one foot (25 cm), and in this way escapes the effects of intense wind blasting in tundra habitats

charcoal   incompletely burned pieces of organic material (usually plant). These are virtually inert and hence become incorporated into lake sediments and peat deposits, where they provide useful indications of former fires. Fine charcoal particles may cause changes in the drainage properties of soils, blocking soil capillaries and leading to waterlogging

chromosome structures in the nucleus of a cell that contain genetic information in the form of DNA

civilization the advancement, refinement, and development of organizational complexity in a society. It is often associated in history with urbanization and the flourishing of education, the arts, and science

climate the average set of weather conditions over a long period in a region

climax the supposed final, equilibrium stage of an ecological succession. Many would question whether real stability in nature is ever achieved

coexistence the capacity of two species to survive alongside each other without harm to either species. Coexistence implies an absence of competition

community an assemblage of different plant and animal species, all found living and interacting together. Although they may give the appearance of stability, communities are constantly changing as species respond in different ways to such environmental alterations as climate change

competition an interaction between two individuals of the same or different species arising from the need of both for a particular resource that is in short supply. Competition usually results in harm to one or both competitors

conservation human protection and enhancement of a habitat or a species

cultivation the management of a soil to increase its fertility, or the management of a plant to increase its productivity

cultural landscape a landscape in which the effects of human activity are strongly evident

cyanobacteria *see* BLUE-GREEN BACTERIA

day length the period from sunrise to sunset. It varies with the season, and this variation acts as a signal for changes in plant and animal behavior, such as flowering and migration respectively

deciduous describing a plant that loses all its leaves during an unfavorable season, which may be particularly cold or particularly dry

decomposition the process by which organic matter is reduced in complexity as microbes use its energy content, usually by a process of oxidation. As living things respire the organic materials and produce carbon dioxide, other elements, such as phosphorus and nitrogen, return to the environment where they are available to living organisms once more. Decomposition is therefore an important aspect of the nutrient cycle

detritivore an animal (usually invertebrate) that feeds upon dead organic matter

DNA deoxyribonucleic acid, the molecule that contains the genetic code

domestication the process of bringing a wild plant or animal into the service of humanity. It often involves the selective breeding and training of the organism

ecosystem an ecological unit of study encompassing the living organisms together with the nonliving environment within a particular habitat

ecotone a boundary region where one type of habitat gradually blends into another

ecotourism tourism to wilderness areas of the world that tries to avoid damaging the environment in its development

eddy turbulence in airflow resulting from the presence of a bluff body

energy budget a comparative "balance sheet" of energy entering and leaving an animal or an ecosystem

energy flow the movement of energy through an ecosystem from sunlight energy fixation in photosynthesis to its acquisition by consumer organisms and its release by respiration

energy output-to-input quotient an expression of the amount of energy derived from a particular agricultural activity compared with the energy invested in it

energy subsidy the additional energy supplied (usually in the form of fossil fuels) for the management of an agricultural ecosystem

erosion the degradation and removal of materials from one location to another, often by means of water or wind

eutrophication an increase of fertility within a habitat, often resulting from pollution by nitrates or phosphate or from the runoff of these materials into water bodies from surrounding land. Although the term most often describes wetland habitats, it can also be applied to terrestrial ecosystems

evaporation the conversion of a liquid to its gaseous phase, particularly the loss of water from terrestrial and aquatic surfaces

evapotranspiration a combination of evaporation from land and water surfaces and the loss of water vapor from plant leaves (transpiration)

evergreen describing a leaf or a plant that remains green and able to photosynthesize throughout the year. Evergreen leaves do eventually fall but may last for several seasons before they do so

fertility in reference to soils, the capacity of a soil to support high plant productivity

fertilizer   a material, either natural or artificial, that when added to the soil can increase the productivity of an agricultural crop

floodplain   the low-lying lands running alongside rivers over which water spreads when it enters a river faster than it can be carried away

food web   the complex interaction of animal feeding patterns in an ecosystem

fossil fuels   energy-rich organic materials, such as coal, oil, and natural gas, used to power domestic and industrial activities

fragility   an expression of the ease with which an organism or a habitat may be damaged. Fragile ecosystems, such as many wetlands, need careful conservation

fragmentation   the division of habitats into smaller and smaller units, often resulting in a loss of biodiversity

genes   the store of hereditary information of living things, which is made up of DNA and is contained within an organism's cells

genetic modification   the alteration of the genetic makeup of an organism using molecular techniques, often the addition of foreign DNA

grazing   the activity of an animal feeding upon the ground-growing herbs in an ecosystem (contrast browsing)

greenhouse effect   the warming of the Earth's surface due to the interaction between radiation and the Earth's atmosphere. Shortwave solar radiation passes through the atmosphere unchanged, but Earth's surface radiates it as long-wave radiation (heat). The atmosphere then absorbs the long-wave radiation as heat because of the presence of greenhouse gases

greenhouse gas   an atmospheric gas that absorbs long-wave radiation and therefore contributes to the warming of the Earth's surface by the greenhouse effect. Greenhouse gases include carbon dioxide, water vapor, methane, chlorofluorocarbons (CFCs), ozone, and oxides of nitrogen

groundwater   water that soaks through soils and rocks, as opposed to water derived directly from precipitation and present on the surface of the soil

growing season   the period of the year that is suitable for the active growth of a plant

habitat   the place where an organism lives

habitat structure   the architecture of vegetation in a habitat. The height and branching patterns of plants contribute to the complexity of vegetation architecture, and this complexity creates microhabitats for animal life

hinterland   the region surrounding and interacting with a city

horticulture   the cultivation of plants for decorative use, as in gardens

humus   the decomposing organic fraction of a soil

hunter-gatherer   one who subsists solely by hunting wild animals and gathering wild plant products. This relatively primitive form of human sustenance involves no agricultural activity

hydrology   the study of the movement of water in its cycles through ecosystems and around the planet

industrialization   a process of change in society in which machinery becomes more important than, and in part replaces, human or animal labor. Historically, it is associated with an increase in fossil-fuel consumption

inertia   the property of resistance to disturbance in an ecosystem. A stable ecosystem is difficult to disturb

interception   a function of plants in which the plant canopy catches rainwater and prevents it from reaching the ground directly

intermediate disturbance hypothesis   the theory that habitats experiencing a low level of disturbance may be richer in species than either heavily disturbed or undisturbed ones

invertebrate   an animal lacking a backbone

ion   a charged element or group of elements (*see* ANION and CATION)

irrigation   the modification of natural water-flow regimes to increase water supply to crop plants

island biogeographic theory   a model that seeks to explain why large, densely spaced patches (or "islands") of a habitat are generally richer in species than small, widely spaced ones

landscape   the general visual layout of an area, containing elements of geology and topography, vegetation, and human artifacts, both agricultural and urban. See also cultural landscape

latitude   imaginary lines drawn hoizontally around the Earth, which are named according to the angle they make with the center of the Earth. Thus, the equator is 0°N or S latitude, and the Poles are 90°N and S. The polar regions thus have higher numbers and are referred to as high latitudes

leaching   the process of removal of ions from soils and sediments as water (particularly acidic water) passes through them

lee   the side of an object sheltered from the wind

lichen   an organism that consists of a combination of an alga or a cyanobacterium with a fungus. The combination may have a leafy form or may look like paint on a rock. Lichens are generally resistant to cold and drought

limestone   sedimentary rocks containing a high proportion of calcium carbonate (lime)

litter   the accumulation of dead (mainly plant) organic material on the surface of a soil

loam   a soil containing a balance of textural elements, clays, silts, and sands

management   the deliberate manipulation of an ecosystem by humans in order to achieve a particular end, such as increased productivity or nature conservation

methane   a gas produced by some living organisms as a result of the incomplete decomposition of organic matter. It is a greenhouse gas, a gas that increases the heat-retention properties of the atmosphere

microbes   microscopic organisms, such as bacteria, fungi, and viruses

microclimate   the small-scale climate within habitats, such as beneath forest canopies or in the shade of rocks. The microclimate is strongly affected by habitat structure

migration   the seasonal movements of animal populations, such as geese, caribou, or plankton

monoculture   the cultivation of an area containing only one species. The term is generally used in reference to crop plants, such as wheat fields

niche   the role that a species plays in an ecosystem. The concept of niche consists of both where the species lives and how it makes its living (such as its feeding requirements, growth patterns, or reproductive behavior)

nitrogen fixation   the process by which certain organisms are able to convert nitrogen gas into organic molecules that can be built into proteins

nonrenewable energy   sources of energy that, once consumed, cannot be replaced, such as fossil fuels

nutrient cycle   the cyclic pattern of element movements between different parts of the ecosystem, together with the balance of input and output to and from the ecosystem

occult precipitation   precipitation that is not registered by a standard rain gauge because it arrives as mist, condensing on surfaces, including vegetation canopies (*see* INTERCEPTION)

organism   any living creature, from bacteria to mammals and plants

overgrazing   the destruction of vegetation that results when pastoral farmers try to maintain a stock density too high to be supported by the primary productivity of a given area

ozone hole   extreme thinning of the stratospheric ozone layer over the polar regions in their respective summers, which allows excessive ultraviolet radiation to reach the Earth's surface. Ozone (O_3) is an unstable form of oxygen gas (O_2)

pastoral   an agricultural activity or land-use system involving the grazing of domestic animals

pathogen   a microbe that is harmful to human health

peat   organic accumulations in wetlands resulting from the incomplete decomposition of vegetation litter

pest   an organism, plant or animal, that interferes with human activities

pesticide   a chemical compound, either natural or artificial in origin, that is toxic to pests and can be used to control their populations

pH   an index of acidity and alkalinity. Low pH means high concentrations of hydrogen ions (hence high acidity), while a high pH indicates strong alkalinity. A pH of 7 indicates neutrality. The pH scale is logarithmic, which means, for instance, that a pH of 4 is ten times as acidic as pH 5

pheromone   a volatile chemical substance produced by an animal as a signal to other members of its species

photosynthesis   the process by which certain organisms trap the energy of sunlight using a colored pigment (usually chlorophyll) and use that energy to take carbon dioxide from the atmosphere and convert it into organic molecules, initially sugars

physiological drought   a condition where water is present in a habitat but is unavailable to a plant, for instance, because it is frozen

pioneer   a species that is an initial colonist in a developing habitat

plate tectonics   the theory that the crust of the Earth is divided into plates, which move over the surface, occasionally colliding and buckling to form mountain chains or deep rifts

podzol   a type of soil, common in the boreal forest (or taiga) zone and in its ecotone with the tundra. It consists of a series of layers formed by the leaching of iron, organic matter, and clay from the upper layers and their deposition lower down

pollen analysis   the identification and counting of fossil pollen grains and spores stratified in peat deposits and lake sediments

pollen grains   cells containing the male genetic information of flowering plants and conifers. The outer coat is robust and survives well in wetland sediments. The distinctive structure and sculpturing of the coats permit their identification even in a fossil form

population   a collection of individual organisms all of the same species

precipitation   aerial deposition of water as rain, dew, snow, or in an occult form, such as the condensation of mist

prehistoric   dating from a time before the advent of written records of human history

primary productivity   the rate at which new organic matter is added to an ecosystem, usually as a result of green plant photosynthesis

radiocarbon dating   a technique for establishing the age of a sample of organic matter, based upon the known decay rate of the isotope 14C (carbon 14)

reclamation   the conversion of a habitat to a condition appropriate for such human activity as agriculture or forestry

rehabilitation   the conversion of a damaged ecosystem back to its original condition

relict   a species or a population left behind following the fragmentation and loss of a previously extensive range

remediation   *see* REHABILITATION

renewable energy   sources of energy that are not exhausted as they are consumed but are automatically replenished, such as hydro, solar, wind, and wave energy

replaceability   the ease with which a particular habitat could be replaced if it were to be lost

resilience   the ability of a stable ecosystem to recover rapidly from disturbance

respiration   the release of energy from organic food materials by a process of controlled oxidation within the cell. Under aerobic conditions carbon dioxide is produced, while anaerobic respiration may lead to the formation of ethyl alcohol

rhizosphere   the region of the soil around a plant root, where the release of organic compounds from the root results in intense microbial activity

salinization   the process by which soils become increasingly salty as water evaporates from their surfaces and dissolved materials are left behind. Soil salinity hinders plant growth and is particularly a problem in dry regions of the world, especially where human irrigation leads to faster evaporation

sediment   material that is deposited within an ecosystem, such as a lake or a peat land, and that accumulates over the course of time. Sediments may be organic and/or mineral in their nature

sedimentation   the process of sediment accumulation

soil structure   the adhesion of soil particles to one another, forming aggregations such as crumbs or blocks

soil texture   the proportions of different particle sizes (clay, silt, sand, gravel) that go to make up the mineral skeleton of the soil (*see also* LOAM)

stability   the capacity of an ecosystem to resist change or to recover rapidly from disturbance

stock density   the density of grazing animals maintained in a pastoral system

stratosphere   the part of the Earth's atmosphere lying above the troposphere, from around nine to 30 miles (15 to 50 km)

succession   the process of ecosystem development. The stages of succession are often predictable as they follow a directional sequence. The process usually involves an increase in the biomass of the ecosystem. Succession is driven by the immigration of new species, environmental alteration, competitive struggles, and eventually some degree of equilibration at the climax stage

sustainable harvest   the harvest of plant or animal products that can be maintained over many seasons without damage to the agricultural ecosystem or loss of productivity

terrestrial   occurring on land

topography   the general form of a landscape, including hills and valleys

transhumance   the seasonal migration of pastoral farmers with their herds between two locations, such as a high altitude for summer grazing and a lower one for winter pasture

transpiration   the loss of water vapor from the leaves of terrestrial plants through the stomata, or pores, in the leaf surface

trophic level   the collection of organisms that occupy a particular stage of the energy flow through an ecosystem, such as primary producer, herbivore, predator, or decomposer

undergrazing   pastoral management in which the stock density is maintained at too low a level to ensure stability. Succession proceeds, often leading to tree and shrub development and the consequent loss of grazing land

urbanization   the development of cities and the migration of people from farmland to cities

vertebrate   an animal with a backbone

watershed   the geographical region from which water drains into a particular stream or wetland (equivalent to catchment). The term is also used to describe the ridge separating two catchments; literally the region where water may be shed in either of two directions

water table   the depth at which water is maintained in the soil of an ecosystem

weathering   the breakdown of rock into smaller particles in soils due to the activity of chemical, physical, and biological processes

weed a plant pest; a plant that grows where people do not wish it to grow

wetland a general term covering all shallow aquatic ecosystems (freshwater and marine) together with marshes, swamps, fens, and bogs

wildlife both the wild animals and wild plants of a habitat

zonation the banding of vegetation along an environmental gradient, such as the transition around a shallow water body from submerged and floating aquatic plants to emergent aquatics, then to reed bed and finally swamp. The concept can also be used in relation to cities, where different zones of the city have different histories and functions

BIBLIOGRAPHY AND FURTHER READING

General bibliography

Archibold, O. W. *Ecology of World Vegetation.* New York: Chapman & Hall, 1995.

Bradbury, Ian K. *The Biosphere.* 2d ed. New York: Wiley, 1998.

Brown, J. H., and M. V. Lomolino. *Biogeography.* 2d ed. Sunderland, Mass.: Sinauer Associates, 1998.

Cox, C. B., and P. D. Moore. *Biogeography: An Ecological and Evolutionary Approach.* 7th ed. Oxford: Blackwell Publishing, 2005.

Gaston, K. J., and J. I. Spicer. *Biodiversity: An Introduction.* 2d ed. Oxford: Blackwell Publishing, 2004.

Landscapes and landscape history

Barbour, M. G., and W. D. Billings, eds. *North American Terrestrial Vegetation.* 2d ed. Cambridge: Cambridge University Press, 2000.

Delcourt, H. R., and P. A. Delcourt. *Quaternary Ecology: A Paleoecological Perspective.* London: Chapman & Hall, 1991.

Forman, R. T. T. *Land Mosaics: The Ecology of Landscapes and Regions.* Cambridge: Cambridge University Press, 1995.

Ingegnoli, V. *Landscape Ecology: A Widening Foundation.* Berlin: Springer, 2002.

Agricultural systems

Ashman, M. R., and G. Puri. *Essential Soil Science.* Oxford: Blackwell Publishing, 2002.

Cronk, Q. C. B., and J. L. Fuller. *Plant Invaders: The Threat to Natural Ecosystems.* London: Earthscan, 2001.

Hengeveld, R. *Dynamics of Biological Invasions.* London: Chapman & Hall, 1989.

Houghton, J. *Global Warming: The Complete Briefing.* 3d ed. Cambridge: Cambridge University Press, 2004.

Mannion, A. M. *Agriculture and Environmental Change.* New York: Wiley, 1995.

Parry, M. *Climate Change and World Agriculture.* London: Earthscan, 1990.

Rosenzweig, C., and D. Hillel. *Climate Change and the Global Harvest: Potential Impacts of the Greenhouse Effect on Agriculture.* Oxford: Oxford University Press, 1998.

Stanhill, G., and H. Z. Enoch, eds. *Greenhouse Ecosystems.* Amsterdam: Elsevier, 1999.

Tivy, J. *Agricultural Ecology.* New York: Wiley, 1990.

Wickens, G. E., N. Haq, and P. Day. *New Crops for Food and Industry.* London: Chapman & Hall, 1989.

Urban systems

Gilbert, O. L. *The Ecology of Urban Habitats.* London: Chapman & Hall, 1989.

Guyot, G. *Physics of the Environment and Climate.* New York: Wiley, 1998.

Hough, M. *Cities and Natural Process.* New York: Routledge, 1995.

Liddle, M. *Recreation Ecology: The Ecological Impact of Outdoor Recreation and Ecotourism.* London: Chapman & Hall, 1997.

Owen, J. *The Ecology of a Garden: The First Fifteen Years.* Cambridge: Cambridge University Press, 1991.

Socolow, R., C. Andrews, F. Berkhout, and V. Thomas. *Industrial Ecology and Global Change.* Cambridge: Cambridge University Press, 1994.

Wheater, C. P. *Urban Habitats.* New York: Routledge, 1999.

History of farms and cities

Delcourt, P. A., and H. R. Delcourt. *Prehistoric Native Americans and Ecological Change: Human Ecosystems in Eastern North America since the Pleistocene.* Cambridge: Cambridge University Press, 2004.

Diamond, J. *Guns, Germs, and Steel.* New York: W. W. Norton, 1999.

Harris, D. R., and G. C. Hillman, eds. *Foraging and Farming: The Evolution of Plant Exploitation.* London: Unwin Hyman, 1989.

Hather, J. G. *Tropical Archaeobotany: Applications and New Developments.* New York: Routledge, 1994.

Lahr, M. M. *The Evolution of Modern Human Diversity.* Cambridge: Cambridge University Press, 1996.

McIntosh, R. J., J. A. Tainter, and S. K. McIntosh, eds. *The Way the Wind Blows: Climate, History, and Human Action.* New York: Colombia University Press, 2000.

Newman, L. F., ed. *Hunger in History: Food Shortage, Poverty, and Deprivation.* Oxford: Basil Blackwell, 1990.

Russell, E. W. B. *People and Land through Time: Linking Ecology and History.* New Haven, Conn.: Yale University Press, 1997.

Simmons, I. G. *Changing the Face of the Earth: Culture, Environment, History.* Oxford: Basil Blackwell, 1989.

WEB SITES

Conservation International

URL: http://www.conservation.org

A site particularly concerned with global biological conservation

Earthwatch Institute

URL: http://www.earthwatch.org

General coverage of environmental problems worldwide

The Food and Agriculture Organization of the United Nations

URL: http://www.fao.org

International coverage of food supply problems

The International Union for the Conservation of Nature

URL: http://www.redlist.org

Many links to other sources of information on particular species, especially those currently endangered

National Parks Service of the United States

URL: http://www.nps.gov

Information on specific conservation problems facing the National Parks

Population Reference Bureau

URL: http://www.prb.org

Global coverage of population problems

Sierra Club

URL: http://www.sierraclub.org

Coverage of general conservation issues in the United States
and also issues relating to farming and land use

United Nations Environmental Program World Conservation Monitoring Center

URL: http://www.unep-wcmc.org

Global statistics on environmental problems

U.S. Census

URL: http://www.census.gov

Population statistics for the United States, with detailed
information on populations in specific regions

U.S. Fish and Wildlife Service

URL: http://www.fws.gov

A valuable resource for information on wildlife conservation

U.S. Geological Survey

URL: http://www.usgs.gov

Coverage of environmental problems affecting landscape
conservation

Note: *Italic* page numbers refer to illustrations.